Daily Encouragement for
THE **SMART**
STEPFAMILY

Books by Ron L. Deal

Daily Encouragement for
THE **SMART**
STEPFAMILY

RON L. DEAL
with Dianne Neal Matthews

BETHANYHOUSE
a division of Baker Publishing Group
Minneapolis, Minnesota

© 2018 by FamilyLife®

Published by Bethany House Publishers
11400 Hampshire Avenue South
Bloomington, Minnesota 55438
www.bethanyhouse.com

Bethany House Publishers is a division of
Baker Publishing Group, Grand Rapids, Michigan

Printed in the United States of America

Library of Congress Cataloging-in-Publication Data
Names: Deal, Ron L., author. | Matthews, Dianne Neal, author.
Title: Daily encouragement for the smart stepfamily / Ron L. Deal with Dianne Neal Matthews.
Description: Bloomington, Minnesota : Bethany House Publishers, [2018]
Identifiers: LCCN 2017038827 | ISBN 9780764230479 (trade paper : alk. paper)
Subjects: LCSH: Families—Religious aspects—Christianity. | Church work with stepfamilies. | Stepfamilies. | Devotional calendars.
Classification: LCC BV4526.3 .D43 2018 | DDC 242/.6—dc23
LC record available at https://lccn.loc.gov/2017038827

Cover design by Eric Walljasper

The authors are represented by MacGregor Literary, Inc.

18   19   20   21   22   23   24   7   6   5   4   3   2   1

Dedication

To Bob and Vicki Maday for passionately extending the dinner invitation.

*To Dennis and Barbara Rainey for accepting the invitation
and then giving blended families a seat at the table.*

And to Bubba and Cindy Cathy for providing the meal.

Acknowledgments

It usually takes a village to write a book. This one is no exception.

This book grew out of the ministries of Smart Stepfamilies™ and FamilyLife®, specifically the daily audio feature *FamilyLife Blended with Ron Deal* that is heard on hundreds of radio stations around the country and online around the world. I'm grateful to the FamilyLife leadership for their vision for this audio feature and the staff (including Keith, Julie, Michelle, Kenny, Justin, and Justin) who serve behind the scenes to make it—and now this book—possible. A special word of thanks goes to my invaluable FamilyLife Blended® team members Nicole Burns and Shannon Simmons for doing more than your fair share of our day-to-day responsibilities and for letting me "cave."

Working with Dianne Neal Matthews has been marvelous. And once again, I'm indebted to Bethany House Publishers, editor Ellen Chalifoux, and agent Chip MacGregor for their countless contributions, all of which are needed if you're going to publish a book.

At the heart of this village is my family. I'm a blessed dad (guys, I love you) and husband (Nan, I love you). I'm humbled by your love and support.

Introduction

Have you got a minute?

In today's fast-paced world that's sometimes hard to come by. If you're like me, you're busy. Kids pull on us this way, career demands that way—even our mobile devices seem to pull on our time and attention. Let's face it, *life* demands. And if we're not careful, our relationships and daily need to once again find True North get lost. And then we get lost.

So, have you got a minute to find your bearings? It's kind of important.

This book has a daily dose of encouragement you can read in a minute or less. It's really not complicated. Your main objective is to glance—just for a minute—at your compass and realign your life and family toward True North. Think of each daily reading as a bit of guidance, inspiration, or challenge to keep you on track. Read the day's thought, reflect on it, and give voice to the prayer. Then try to carry one point, one application, or one insight with you into your day.

I suggest you:

- Start where you are. Look up today's date and start reading.
- Read each entry as a couple. But don't fret; if life gets in the way, read individually and briefly discuss it later if you can.

- Share one or two per week with your children, perhaps over dinner or while driving in the car. Bring them into your faith journey so you can help shape theirs. There's another reason to do this: regularly bringing family members together around God's truth aids in the bonding process of your blended family. Over time this can build family harmony. One more thought: Be discerning about which entries you pick or which part you share based on the ages of your children and the strength of your relationship. Don't force the material; just go with what makes sense in this season of your family life.

- Don't let guilt throw you off track. If you miss a day . . . or week, don't be defeated. Just turn to the current day's entry and start again.

As someone who has studied and worked intimately with stepfamilies for over twenty-five years, I can assure you that blended families are complex creatures; not every page in this book will apply to your family. But I hope that each day you'll be able to find a nugget that does apply. If not, say a prayer for the family to whom it does pertain. Maybe the next day they'll be praying for you.

Want more? These thoughts are based on my one-minute audio feature called *FamilyLife Blended*, which is available on hundreds of radio outlets nationwide and on social media. Find hundreds more daily doses of inspiration at our website, *familylifeblended.com*.

New Year's Resolution

How's this for a resolution for the year ahead: "Set your minds on things that are above" (Colossians 3:2).

Regardless of the goal, the first step is to set our minds to it. Our Creator knows how we're wired. He understands what it takes to bring about change in our lives. Whatever we think about or dwell on is what we tend to become.

Imagine telling a child, "Don't spill your milk." Guess what that child is thinking about now? You just made it more likely that the milk will hit the floor. A better comment would be something like, "Walk slowly and hold your glass with two hands." Now you have set their mind on the desired outcome.

The same principle applies to you and your goals. So why not put Colossians 3:2 at the top of your list of resolutions? Of course, setting your mind on the things of God is always a good mindset any day of the year, but you might as well start today.

Lord, as I think about personal and family goals for the coming year, I ask you to keep my focus on things that have eternal value rather than temporary earthly pursuits.

Learn All You Can

My first piece of advice for stepfamilies is always this: Learn all you can about healthy stepfamily living. Sure, your general knowledge of marriage and parenting will prove helpful, but it's the unique dynamics of stepfamily living that create stress and end up dividing families. So the smarter you are about relationships in *your* home, the better equipped you are to nurture and manage them.

Seek out resources specifically developed for the blended family. Although advice meant for biological parents may sometimes be helpful, in some cases it can actually backfire on stepparents. You'll have far more success with resources designed for the blended family home with all its unique circumstances and challenges—and yes, all its wonderful blessings, too.

Getting "stepfamily smart" is the beginning of a successful stepfamily.

Father, you know the needs of our family even better than we do. Please lead us to the best resources that will help us understand how to build a strong, healthy family that honors you and blesses those around us.

A Rose
by Any Other Name

Ron, I've been a stepparent for fifteen years now. When is it going to happen?"

There's something special about the labels *Mom* and *Dad*. No wonder stepparents long to hear those words. It doesn't seem like it would be a big deal; after all, stepparents often say "my kids" when referring to their stepchildren. Why is it so hard for kids to reciprocate? The fact is, only about one-third will call their stepparent Mom or Dad. Kids are fiercely loyal to their biological parents, and they don't want to risk hurting their feelings.

The best approach is to relax and not force the issue. Labels are not what matter most; your role in the child's life is. The sense of being protected and loved that you instill. The growing bond of trust and appreciation. The privilege of nurturing a unique individual created by God. In the end, the label won't matter; the love will.

Heavenly Father, show me how to parent each of my children with love and wisdom. Even if my stepchild never calls me by the name I long to hear, remind me that what matters in the long run is our relationship and my faithfulness to it.

Go Ahead— Think Out Loud!

Want an easy, effective way to develop your child's faith? Think out loud. In other words, share with your kids how you reached a certain decision. For example, let's say you decided *not* to buy something for yourself because you felt it more Kingdom-minded to use the money another way. Next time you're in the car, think out loud: "Hey buddy, we decided not to buy that four-wheeler. We wrestled with it but decided to use the money for a service project instead. We believe this honors God and buying another thing for ourselves doesn't."

Verbalizing your decision-making process shapes your child's faith by showing how life and faith interconnect. What a powerful way to instill godly principles and priorities in your kids. Plus, there's an added bonus for stepparents: When you think out loud, you're inviting your stepchild to peek into your heart. And each vulnerable glimpse you offer helps them see you more clearly and trust your heart more.

Help me think about your goodness, your mercy, and your power all day long. And never let me pass up a chance to think out loud about you, especially around my family.

Act Your Best

A ct your best!"
Ever hear those words from your mom? You know, it's really not bad advice. But have you ever noticed how you naturally act your best whenever you're meeting someone for the first time? Maybe you'd been in the worst mood ever moments before, or acted unpleasantly toward a loved one. Now suddenly you have a big smile on your face and you're gushing all sweetness as you're introduced to someone new. Why do we do that?

Maybe it's because we want to make a good first impression. Or maybe we take family members for granted since we figure they're not going anywhere. But permanence of the relationship is no excuse for bad behavior. Remember how you treated that waitress at lunch? Be just as kind and polite toward your spouse. And treat your kids with just as much patience as your co-workers. Make an effort to always act your best, but especially toward those you love most.

Lord, please keep me from falling into the trap of taking family members for granted. Remind me to always be on my best behavior with my loved ones, treating them with the same respect and kindness I show others.

Traveling by Alternate Routes

There's something unique about stepfamily dynamics: Everyone in the blended family living room traveled a different journey to get there. In a nuclear family everyone shares the same family story. But stepfamilies include individuals with different family histories, different DNA, different outlooks, traditions—a different culture. Merging those cultures can prove difficult.

To cross the gaps in your family stories, you've got to build bridges of communication.

Have family members talk about cherished holiday traditions they find meaningful. Ask your stepchild what it feels like to be the oldest child in one home and a middle child in another. Share how past hurts have changed who you are today; invite your children to do the same.

Ignoring how different backgrounds have impacted family members can lead to misunderstandings, resentment, and conflict. It's crucial to handle these differences with honest communication and a healthy dose of unconditional acceptance. Such an atmosphere will ensure that no matter what route brought each person into your family, all are content with their destination.

Please show me how each family member has been affected by past experiences. Help me set an example of honest communication and loving acceptance of our differences.

Never Stop Learning

When I married my wife more than three decades ago, I was really dumb! Not dumb as in *stupid*, but dumb as in *naïve*. I had no clue about all the things I needed to learn to do or say, the skills I'd need to develop to be a good husband. I also had no idea that our "us-ness" would require sacrifices from me I never knew I would have to give.

When you think about it, not knowing what lay ahead was really a gift from God. If we had known all that would be required of us, we might have hesitated to sign on the dotted line of the marriage license. But we couldn't see the future then, and we still can't. We only have to trust God and always be ready and willing to be taught. Thankfully, even when we're clueless, God knows exactly what we need to learn.

Holy Spirit, thank you for being my teacher and counselor. Give me the understanding I need in order to love and honor my spouse in ways that strengthen our relationship and equip us to face whatever challenges the future holds.

Don't Expect Perfection

Have you ever searched through the Bible to find a model family to emulate? Well, I have. And guess what? I didn't find one. Sure, God's perfect plan for the family is all laid out in Scripture. But we can't find one family in its pages that lived out his plan perfectly. Not a single one. And instead of being discouraged about that, I've decided it's not such a bad thing.

You see, I find great encouragement in reading about the sibling rivalry between Cain and Abel, about Abraham's failings as a husband, and about Jacob's messed-up blended brood. It's not exactly their imperfections that encourage me; it's the fact that in spite of their miserable failings, God called them, redeemed them, used them, and matured them. In the end, he counted them as righteous.

Thankfully, that same redemption is available for my imperfect family—and for yours as well.

Thank you, Lord, for your willingness to use imperfect people. Help each member of our family grow in godliness, knowing that your mercy covers all our shortcomings and failures.

To Speak or Not to Speak

Family life is sweeter when parents are on the same side. But a biological parent in a stepfamily walks a precarious tightwire: They know they need to back up the stepparent, yet sometimes feel the need to speak up for their child. How can you resolve this awkward situation to everyone's benefit?

First, make sure your kids understand that while you have their best interests at heart, you fully support their stepparent. That doesn't mean you have to step in and play therapist every time your child and spouse disagree. Sometimes it's best to let the two parties figure it out on their own.

Still, there will be times when you have to say something tough to your spouse. Always speak in private. Open the conversation along this line: "Because I want to support you, I'd like to share my thoughts about what's happening." Make your loyalty clear *before* you offer your personal perspective. After all, moving toward your spouse is the first step to helping your spouse move toward your children.

Father, give me wisdom to know when to speak up and when to shut up. Help me use words that promote unity and peace in our family.

How to Befriend a Squirrel

So how *do* you befriend a squirrel anyway? I'm directing that question to anyone who wants to fix a relationship—with a friend, family member, or spouse—but the other person doesn't want to. It's like trying to make friends with a squirrel, isn't it? You can't chase it because it just runs away. It does no good to complain, nag, or yell at it. Trying to trap it is a waste of time because catching it just makes it even more afraid.

To befriend a squirrel, you have to sit in the park with something the squirrel considers desirable . . . and wait. And wait. And wait some more. You can't make the squirrel want to come near you unless you have something enticing to offer.

So if you're the only one interested in repairing a relationship, the best approach is to take on the character of Christ. His spirit of gentleness, mercy, and grace that drew people to him. The kind of spirit that invites reconciliation. Do your part; the rest is up to the squirrel.

Jesus, fill me with your spirit of gentleness and grace so that the door to reconciliation stays wide open.

Break Down the Wall

F inally, I let myself love again."

Sometimes when people go through a significant breakup, they think twice about loving again with their whole heart. Carissa shared with us on Facebook that she built a huge wall around her heart after her first husband changed for the worse, leading to a divorce. When she remarried, she assumed that the same thing would happen with her second husband. She *expected* to be disappointed.

But Carissa's new husband didn't disappoint her, and after a while she realized that her wall was still up. It had to come down. She understood the problem with walls. Building a wall around your heart can protect you from hurt, but it also prevents you from fully loving another person—which ironically makes it more likely that you will get hurt again.

Take a moment to check the terrain of your own heart. If you find even the beginnings of a wall, find courage as Carissa did. Break down your wall, trust God, and let yourself love—and be loved.

Give me the strength and courage to tear down any walls that block me from loving someone else with my whole heart.

Adopting Outsiders

D o you know what it's like to be adopted? Some of you do. Most, like me, have no idea. Then again, if we follow Christ we do know about adoption in one sense. The Bible reminds us in Romans 3 that sin made us outsiders to God, separated from him because of our sin. Christ's sacrifice, however, made it possible for God to adopt us as his children (Romans 8:15–17).

Imagine what would happen if we all passed that on—if we opened up our hearts to an outsider and invited them in. A lonely kid on the playground would have a friend. A new extended blended family member would be treated as if they belong. Someone with a different skin color or accent would be welcome in your living room. And a newcomer to church would receive five invitations to lunch.

God reached across the seemingly insurmountable obstacle of sin and adopted us as his children. Now let's go out and adopt someone in that same spirit.

Father, open up my heart to outsiders who need to be adopted.
Lead me to someone who needs your loving touch today.

Share the Real You

Let me share something ironic: In today's world we're more connected than we've ever been before—and we're also more disconnected than ever.

If you look around, you'll notice that envy and jealousy seem to be at an all-time high. Why? Because the daily highlight reel of social media makes everyone else's life look perfect and wonderful. So while we're more connected to other people's lives, we distance ourselves in envy because our lives just don't measure up to theirs.

The only way to truly connect, both *within* your family and *between* families, is through transparency—honestly sharing your true self rather than your sanitized social media persona. Why not try it yourself and see the difference it makes? For example, find the courage to share the good, the bad, and the ugly of your spiritual journey with a friend or family member. Give them a chance to love the real you. And see if they don't return the favor.

Lord, forgive me when I compare my life with someone else's and end up feeling envious. Help me be willing to honestly share my disappointments and struggles and to encourage others to do the same.

Blendering:
A Big Mistake

Watch out—don't start blendering! (Okay, I admit it; I like to make up words.) *Blendering* is my created word for what couples do to force their blended family to blend. You see, blenders make ingredients collide with intense force until they combine and meld into each other. That's fine when making smoothies, but not helpful when dealing with children and family relationships.

Blendering demands that deep love and affection develop quickly between stepfamily members, and then sets out to make it happen on the adult's time frame. There's a lot of pressure in that. Ever had a desperate person pressure you to love them back? That attitude pushes you away, doesn't it?

So relax. Stop blendering; instead have Crockpot expectations. Let ingredients warm up to one another, slowly and in their own time. I promise you'll be more pleased with the results. Believe me, blendering in blended families is a blunder you do not want to make.

Heavenly Father, help me accept the truth that deep, loving relationships take time to develop. Show me how to relax and let go of any unrealistic expectations that make others feel pressured.

More or Less, Part 1

Does God's Word offer practical advice about how we should live on a day-to-day basis? Yes it does, more or less. By *more or less*, I don't mean that the Bible *vaguely* describes how we should live; I mean it advises us to do *more* of some things and *less* of others. For example, Colossians 3 includes a list of things we should do more of—like being kind and forgiving toward one another (vv. 12–15). It also lists things we should do less of—like lying or harboring anger or malice in our minds (vv. 5–11).

And really, that's where it all starts: with our thoughts. The first two verses of this chapter advise us to set our hearts and minds on things above, not on earthly things. In other words, focus on Christ and what it means to live for him. Why not give that a try right now? Spend the next two minutes considering how you might spend the rest of your day loving God and loving others—in a "more or less" fashion.

Lord Jesus, keep my thoughts fixed on you as I look for opportunities to love and serve those who cross my path today.

More or Less, Part 2

Yesterday we talked about how Colossians 3 urges us to do more of some things and less of others. The chapter also offers a list of character and behavioral traits we should "put on" or "clothe" ourselves with: compassion, kindness, humility, meekness, and patience (v. 12). At the same time, it urges us to "put away" anger, malice, slander, obscene talk, and lying (vv. 8–9).

Notice how these two lists differ from each other? That first list calls us to be other-focused. It moves us outside of ourselves and has us consider the needs of others. The list of traits to avoid is self-focused, making us absorbed in what we want or what we can get from others. Two polar-opposite lifestyles—and every day we choose which one to follow.

To walk with Christ and to build a stronger family, we need to make some changes, more or less, to the focus of our lives: more on others and less on self.

Jesus, help me clothe myself with your character traits so that I can live the selfless, sacrificial lifestyle you modeled throughout your earthly ministry.

More or Less, Part 3

Today let's wrap up our look at the "more or less" approach to living found in Colossians 3. To our list of things we're to do more of, let's add forgiving others, just as the Lord has forgiven us, and being filled with peace in our interactions toward others. As a finishing touch, we're urged to put on love, which will bind all the other virtues together in perfect harmony (vv. 13–15).

Things we are to do less of: being angry, raging at others, speaking poorly about people or intending to do evil toward them, lying to others or using crude language (vv. 8–9). Essentially then, more or less, we are called to stop doing things that pit us *against* others and instead be *for* them.

That might sound like a tall order in light of the difficult people around us who don't care about the lists in Colossians 3. If so, stop and think about all that Christ endured and suffered so that God can be *for* us. Doesn't that make it easier?

Lord, in light of all you suffered for me, help me be willing to forgive freely, love deeply, and spread peace generously.

Give It Some Time

Expecting too much too soon in a new stepfamily can lead to misunderstandings, resentment, and even disaster. One common pitfall in this area is expecting the stepparent and the stepkids to become affectionate with each other right away. Sometimes this seems to happen naturally, and that's great when it does. But more often than not, it's a process that takes time. Maybe a long time.

Here's one solution: pay close attention to your stepchild's level of affection with you, and then match it. Find out what gestures they prefer, whether a kiss, hug, wink, wrestle, high-five, or fist bump—whatever, and go with that. Let that be enough for today, trusting that tomorrow might open the door to something new and deeper.

When it comes to stepparenting, taking small steps gets you farther down the road than forcing big strides.

Help me be content with the depth of relationships in our blended family, remembering to value the uniqueness of each family member. Teach me the best ways to show love and acceptance to each one of my stepchildren.

Attitude Adjustments

Ron, I'm an adult and my mom is dating a guy. And I'm having a rough time with it."

I once heard from someone who was struggling with her mom's engagement. "My dad died five years ago," she said. "And even though I'm happy for my mom, I'm not comfortable with their relationship. But I am trying to be supportive."

No matter how old you are, when a parent dates or marries, it dramatically changes your life in unwanted ways. But I do appreciate this woman's attitude. She's at least trying to be supportive . . . to be welcoming . . . understanding . . . selfless.

Her mom needs to try, too. Try to understand how a new person in her life has vast implications for her adult child. And try to be patient . . . understanding . . . and selfless.

These attitudes are admirable, but they don't make all the necessary adjustments easy. Having the right attitude is only one part of the solution. But it does bring grace to the equation. And grace always helps, no matter what situation or challenge you're facing.

Lord, help me approach each relationship and family change with an attitude of understanding and support. May every person who enters our home feel welcomed and surrounded by grace.

Permission Granted

Ron, I'm concerned. My children now have a stepparent in their other home, and I'm afraid I'm going to lose them. What do I do?"

I can appreciate this mom's struggle. Her children now have a stepmom. She's worried that if she gives her kids permission to like or love their stepmom, it might somehow take away from her relationship with them.

Well, I have good news for anyone with similar concerns. I don't care how fond your child becomes of a stepparent, you will never lose your significance in your child's heart. Biological parents and children have an incomparable, God-given, DNA-deep bond that cannot be replaced. So giving them permission—and even encouragement—to like, love, and obey their stepparent in the other home takes nothing away from you. Plus it blesses them.

Rest assured that your children have more than enough love for everybody—and so do you.

Father, thank you for the special bond I have with my child. Please give me the grace to encourage healthy, loving relationships with their other set of parents without worrying that it might detract from what we have.

January 21

Watch Out for Ambition

Ambition can be a dangerous thing. Does that sound strange? After all, what could be so bad about striving to achieve your goals, wanting to come out on top? There's the problem: Relying on yourself and taking matters into your own hands is a subtle act of becoming your own god. It chips away at your awareness of your need for the true God.

In Psalm 131:2 David writes, "I have calmed and quieted my soul [or ambition]." If we're not careful, ambition can make us independent of God, which leads to pride. Maybe you listed a few resolutions on New Year's Day. That list can be a useful tool to help you focus your efforts, but if your goals are fueled by ambition they'll pull you away from God.

David offers a better option; he encourages us to trust God and be content with what he provides. So how about your ambitions for your family? Are you trusting God, or taking measures into your own hands?

"O Lord, my heart is not lifted up; my eyes are not raised too high"(Psalm 131:1). May my goals and dreams never take priority over my relationship with you.

Safely Navigating the Minefield

Attorney Joseph Kniskern calls stepfamilies a "monetary minefield."[1] And he's right. There's complexity to blended-family relationships, and there's also complexity to managing money in a blended family. That's partly because family law gives preference to blood relationships and marriage.

For example, as a stepparent you may have a wonderful relationship with your stepchildren, but if your spouse—their biological parent—dies, custody will go to the other biological parent, not to you. Unless you've formally adopted your stepchildren you don't have any parental rights.

Given these kinds of legal considerations, let me encourage you to consult an attorney and create a written agreement outlining your wills, estate plan, and financial and parenting plans. Blended family finances may be a minefield, but with the right help you *can* avoid the mines.

Father, grant us wisdom and lead us to the best resources for handling our family finances and planning for the future.

Guard Your Family Time

Research confirms that spending time together is a hallmark of strong, healthy families. But in today's world, finding time to be together can be a real challenge. There's so much stuff competing for our time and attention. Instant downloads, instant entertainment, and—thanks to cell phones—virtual conversations competing with live ones at the dinner table.

Stepfamilies have even greater challenges in this area: children who move between homes, numerous grandparents who lobby for time with the grandkids, parents who move far away, and sometimes uninvolved parents. If you want to be a strong family, you've got to find ways around these barriers.

Resolve not to let smartphones interrupt family dinnertime, but use that same technology to stay in touch with family members. And be proactive to manage the activities schedule of your home. Don't lose track of time, or you might lose track of each other.

> *Help us find creative ideas to manage situations and influences that weaken the closeness of our relationships. Renew our commitment to guard our family time with each other.*

Honor the Past While Looking Ahead

amily is a link to the past and a bridge to the future.

We hear a lot of people talking about their family tree these days, don't we? That's not surprising since the Internet has provided tools that make exploring our ancestry so much easier. Researching our history tells us who we are and where we came from.

Now here's a blended family trap: Sometimes the adults are so focused on where the new family is going that they inadvertently step on the children's past. When a stepparent *demands* a child call them Mom or Dad, it feels like they are pruning limbs off the family tree. Or when a family tradition that has been shared by some is pushed aside by new stepfamily members, it squashes something in a child.

To truly be a bridge to the future, your stepfamily needs to honor the past, not try to erase it.

Lord, remind us to honor our children's past history by acknowledging all branches of our family tree, the original ones as well as those recently grafted in.

Never Give Up

Are you struggling in your marriage? You're not alone—many couples are struggling with some aspect of their relationship. It might help to take a lesson from successful stepfamily couples. While research reveals there is no single factor that predicts stability in stepcouple marriages, we can identify three things successful couples do: They work hard at communicating effectively. They persist in problem-solving; when they get stuck, they change how they approach the problem until they find a solution. And they deal with larger family issues, such as stepparenting.[2]

The bottom line is that although successful couples have just as many conflicts, they refuse to quit until they find a way through. When a couple divorces, that means somebody gave up trying. Let me urge you not to fall into that category. God made you to be an overcomer. Your marriage is worth fighting for. With his help, stay the course.

Heavenly Father, help us learn to communicate well, to creatively solve problems as a team, and to deal with family issues as they arise.

Let God Be in Charge

Sometimes when we're "grasping at straws," what we're really trying to grab hold of is control. People in tough situations often write to me hoping I can tell them how to gain control of their lives. This tendency points out one of the hardest aspects of the faith-centered life: trusting God.

Think about it for a minute. Ask these same people about their past, and chances are they'll share stories about how God provided for their needs and took care of them. But then ask them about the future—about their marriage, their kids, their retirement. Most likely, their first inclination is to try to figure it out all by themselves.

I understand the struggle. When asked about my future I want to have an answer. But what I know deep down is that I'm much better off not having all the answers. Life is better when I simply trust God and allow myself to be dependent on him rather than grasping for control.

Lord, I'm tired of trying to control circumstances and people rather than resting in your sovereignty. I release my family and my future into your loving hands.

Be Like Jesus

When you're faced with a difficult person, be like Jesus. By that I mean be as loving as you can be while speaking and living out truth as he did. Let's face it, we all have difficult people in our lives, and so do our kids. That could be another child at school or our next-door neighbor. For some divorced Christians it's the biological parent in the other home. This can be an especially tough situation. Even though you understand their rightful place in your child's life, you might not appreciate their influence.

So what do you do? Here's a starting point: Set a good example. You may not be able to control someone else's behavior, but with God's help you can certainly control your own. See each new day as an opportunity to grow and strive to be more like Jesus. And when you feel disappointed in other people's behavior, remember that light always outshines the darkness.

Examine my heart, God, and show me thoughts, attitudes, and habits that do not honor you. Use every person and situation in my life to make me more like Christ and reflect his light.

Cooperate for Your Kids' Sake

If you're a divorced parent, then please—for the sake of your child—do everything you can to cooperate with the other home. There's no question that having divorced parents leaves children with a few bumps and bruises. But long-term, kids tend to fare reasonably well if their parents put differences and animosity aside in order to cooperate on the child's upbringing.

In contrast, the more parents argue or fight, the more wounded their kids will be. An old African proverb observes, "When two elephants fight, it's the grass that suffers." It's been my experience that divorced parents intuitively know this, and yet most of them still engage their ex in a cold or angry war.

Remember that co-parenting is not about you. It's about what's best for your kids. And for you to manage it well, you may have to forgive the past and set aside what you consider fair. For the sake of your kids, you can do this. You have to do this.

Father, I ask you to help me release old grudges, to heal old wounds, and to fill our hearts and homes with your forgiveness and peace.

The Value of Time Divided

Most stepfamilies are working hard to connect and bond with each other. So is it ever okay to leave someone out? Essentially that was the question a sixty-two-year-old woman recently asked me. Her email explained that she and her husband both have adult children and grandchildren from previous marriages. She loves being with his side of the family, but sometimes she wants to go visit her grandkids while her husband is working.

Personally, I believe that compartmentalizing your time and relationships like this can be healthy for stepfamilies. Spending exclusive time with your family renews and refreshes the hearts of those who have suffered a fracturing of their family. Of course, it's important to keep everything in balance. Make sure you give time to new relationships and to the entire stepfamily as well as your own. But if handled correctly, a little biological family time is a nice respite for everyone.

Show me the best way to divide my time and attention between our families. Help us create an atmosphere of openness and acceptance so that family members are comfortable discussing any feelings of being slighted or overlooked.

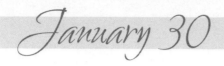

Develop God-Esteem

It's true that having a healthy self-esteem is a good thing. But there is something far better. Self-esteem is essentially about accepting yourself and having confidence in your worth and abilities. On the other hand, God-esteem isn't based on what you think of yourself; it's rooted in how heaven sees you. It stems from how God is growing and shaping you.

In Christ, you are forgiven and loved unconditionally. You are a precious child of the King whose story of imperfection is being redeemed into God's perfect story for the world. Your life has worth and value beyond compare because of what Christ has done and the work he is doing in you.

Now, what if you reacted to others on the basis of how God views you? Critical words wouldn't hurt quite as bad. Imperfections wouldn't threaten you as deeply. The approval of others wouldn't matter nearly as much. And you could love in spite of them all, freely and fully the way God loves you.

God, each time I look in the mirror, remind me that my reflection is not nearly as important as how you see me.

January 31

The Power
of a Humble Spirit

Proverbs 6 lists seven things the Lord hates. And the first item on the list is pride ("haughty eyes," v. 17). Throughout the Scriptures, God makes it clear that he will oppose and bring low those who think highly of themselves. But it's also clear that those who keep a humble spirit, who consider others first and seek to love and serve them, will be lifted up and granted mercy.

Let me encourage you today to remain humble before the Lord—but don't stop there. Ask him to help you be humble about who you are with others. Whether interacting with a husband, wife, child, parent, sibling, or friend, "do nothing from selfish ambition or conceit, but in humility count others more significant than yourselves" (Philippians 2:3).

Now just imagine if everyone in your family lived that way. How would the atmosphere in your home be different?

Remove any traces of self-centered pride from my heart, Lord. In all my interactions with family members and friends, let me put their needs and welfare above my own.

Key Steps for Steps, Part 1

Ron, our marriage is great. It would be wonderful if it were just he and I, but it's not."

This statement from Sarah shows that she has come to realize an important truth: the job of parenting dramatically affects a stepfamily marriage. For the next five days, let's review some key steps for stepfamilies first outlined in my book *The Smart Stepfamily*. Today's suggestion is: Step in line.

As you probably know, a line dance is when a number of people stand beside each other and do the same dance steps. This is something blended families need to imitate. All the adults, sometimes across many homes, need to coordinate their parenting as much as they can in order to bring harmony to the parenting process. This helps kids grow in a healthy environment, and it helps couples have a stronger marriage.

No, cooperation isn't easy. But when it does happen, everything else gets better. So for the sake of your marriage and family, don't sit this one out. Make sure you step in line.

Help me infuse a spirit of cooperation into every interaction I have with biological and stepfamily members alike.

Key Steps for Steps, Part 2

N o, we can't have you at our church because your background and past might infect everyone else."

Can you imagine a pastor saying that to you—or to anybody? But it did happen. Essentially the pastor told this couple, "Because you're a blended family, you are barred from coming to our church." This incident leaves me wondering, *Where in the world did we get the idea that you have to be perfect before you can come to Christ? Isn't that what he does for us?*

Today's recommended key step for stepfamilies is this: Step up . . . to discover a God who loves and forgives those in blended families. Let's be honest and admit that some stepfamilies *are* the result of sinful choices, while others are not. But either way, Christ welcomes you to his body. He promises to wash you clean and give you a fresh start.

With such a loving Savior waiting, who wouldn't want to step up for that?

Lord Jesus, please open the eyes of every member of our family to see and accept the great sacrifice you made that allows us to stand before you forgiven and cleansed from all sin.

Key Steps for Steps, Part 3

Okay, stepfamilies, it's time to step down. Step down your expectations, that is. "Why won't my son ask his stepfather for help with his math?" one mom asked me. "Tim is a lot better at it than I am." You see, this mom just wanted her son to feel comfortable with Tim, so she kept pressuring them to get along. But as is often the case, the pressure only backfired.

When you step down your expectations, that does not mean you're giving up. It just means that you understand the fact that family integration, as I like to call it, takes time. Many years for most families. Pressure does nothing at all to help speed up the process; in fact, it usually thwarts relationships that would naturally develop on their own.

Accepting and appreciating step-relationships just as they are today makes for a more relaxed home—and that, ironically, helps people become family.

Help me resist the temptation to speed up the process of blending our family members together according to my expectations, and instead simply enjoy each individual as much as I can as they are right now.

Key Steps for Steps, Part 4

The two-step is not just a dance in Texas; it's something far more important than that. In any home, the marriage relationship is by far the most important earthly relationship. Yet in blended families, it's often the most vulnerable. In light of this fact, my key step for today is: Do the two-step—in your marriage, that is.

Single parents and their children have been through an awful lot together. Surviving in the foxhole of life makes loyalties strong. For that reason, making the marriage a relational priority can be tough to manage. But that doesn't make it any less crucial to the family's growth and success. It's got to become the new backbone for the family.

The marital dance is about you—and about balancing time and energy given to the kids. But ultimately, everyone needs to know that the marriage is unbreakable, and that the couple will lead the home together. So figure out how you can make your marital two-step your number one priority.

Lord, help me always remember that my relationship with my spouse takes highest priority after you, and that our marriage is to be cherished and valued as something sacred.

Key Steps for Steps, Part 5

Most of us have a wilderness or two to cross at some point in our lives. And like Moses and the Israelites headed for the Promised Land, sometimes it takes us a lot longer to get to our destination than we would like. During those times, all we can do is focus on stepping through the wilderness with trust and raw determination.

Stepfamilies have to "step through" their wilderness, too. They'll reach the Promised Land when they've had time to create a family identity and smooth out the bumps in the newly formed relationships. And because that journey can take a while, it's really important to keep on trusting God to provide direction. We must stay determined not to look back at Egypt, but to keep our eyes fixed on what lies ahead.

Yes, there is a Promised Land for stepfamilies—and it's well worth the effort to get there.

Help us keep our eyes focused on what lies ahead for our family and our hearts fixed on the hope of your promises as we journey through life together.

Pick Your Battles

Sometimes the best way to work out a disagreement is not to work it out at all, but to drop it. Mind you, I'm not talking here about avoiding a subject or conversation that needs to take place. In those cases, avoiding the issue doesn't resolve anything; it simply postpones the conflict. What I am suggesting is that not every single thing is worth confrontation. Sometimes it's best to be generous with mercy and just let it go.

"The start of a quarrel is like a leak in a dam, so stop it before it bursts." (Proverbs 17:14 THE MESSAGE paraphrase). Let's keep in mind that not every dispute is a hill to die on, especially if your marriage or family is already stressed. So whenever you can, just let it go. Sometimes shutting an eye does everyone a favor. And who knows, that might actually help you see things more clearly.

Father, I need your wisdom to know when to let go and when to confront. During times of disagreement, help me speak graciously and calmly.

How Big Is Your Heart?

Some people are easy to love, and others—not so much. I guess it depends on how big your heart is. I once met a couple who lead a stepfamily small group in their church alongside his ex-wife and her new husband. Yes, you heard me right. They co-teach the program—*together.* And they do it successfully.

The real story is how they got to this point. Despite not getting along, the stepmom felt prompted by the Holy Spirit to buy her husband's ex-wife a holiday gift. Eventually, this big-hearted act of love paid off and the two women became friends. Since then, all relationships on both sides have dramatically improved. Even to the point of co-teaching a class about marriage and family—together.

Having a big heart is essentially a choice we make to move past petty insecurities, to stop building walls, to soften our hearts, and to obey God. Once we make that choice, surprising things can happen.

Heavenly Father, help me make the choices that will allow my heart to grow so that I can love others the way you do.

Bonus Love

Okay, Ron, just where do I fit in this picture?"

I heard this familiar question while talking with a friend of mine. He's a stepdad and he loves his kids dearly. He said, "Ron, I want to be the one who teaches my stepson how to shave and the one who walks Emily down the aisle on her wedding day, but I think their dad ought to do those things. So what is my role?"

You know, being the bonus mom or dad sometimes means you don't get the first seat at the table (and you'll have to grieve this). But it does mean that as an added parent figure in the life of a child, everything you offer is a bonus! A bonus hug, a bonus word of encouragement, a bonus smile, a bonus challenge, a bonus godly influence. And in a world where some people don't have any at all—bonus love. Doesn't that have a nice ring to it? When you think about it in that light, being a bonus parent is a great role to fill.

Dear God, never let me take for granted the privilege and honor of being a bonus blessing in the lives of my stepchildren.

A Crockpot Family

What do you get when you combine two families and playtime? Dinner! Okay, I probably need to explain that. Here's a suggestion for a family activity: Assemble all the ingredients for a Crockpot meal and then gather your family members in the kitchen. Have each person add one ingredient to the slow cooker while you talk about how stepfamilies come together.

"Each of us," you might say, "is a part of this dish. We may enter the pot uncooked, but over time love warms our hearts and we come together. But remember how a Crockpot takes many hours to cook a meal? Well, our family may take a long time to combine well, but eventually we're going to taste really good! And each ingredient—each of us—is really important to the dish. We all have something to contribute to the outcome."

When you do this activity with your kids, you'll give them more than just dinner; you'll provide a visual illustration that will stick in their minds long after the food is gone.

Father, show me how to make sure that each family member knows they are a vital ingredient in our special family dish.

A Redeemed Story

Is your life story less than perfect? Join the club. In John 4 Jesus encounters a woman at a village well who needs water. Married five times and now living with another man, she's been thirsty for a long time—and for more than just water. What does Jesus offer her? Living water, along with a redeemed life. And that changes everything.

This woman, who had previously avoided social interaction because of her shame, goes out and becomes an evangelist for Jesus. She uses her messed-up life as evidence of his redeeming power, bringing others to receive his life-giving water.

Here is that woman's message to you: You can't change your imperfect past. But you can allow God to wrap your imperfect story into his perfect story of redemption. And you can share with someone what he's done for you. Then, like that woman at the well so long ago, maybe they too can come out of hiding.

Jesus, we invite you to weave our imperfect family's story into your larger plan of redemption. Give us the boldness to point those around us to you as the only source of living water.

No Second-Class Christians

feel like the church's dirty little problem."

Sad to say, I've heard this remark many, many times. John explained that after his divorce he didn't think he could go back to church again. Now he's happy to be remarried and part of a blended family, yet he feels like a second-class Christian.

Admittedly, it's possible that John's feelings are actually rooted in conviction over something that he needs to repent of and seek forgiveness for. But if it's solely his church that's making him feel second-class, then something is wrong. Dreadfully wrong. After all, there's no such thing as a second-class Christian, because there is no such thing as a *first-class* Christian. We're all just sinners in need of the Cross.

Do you sometimes feel "less than" because of your past? If so, fall into the grace of God and seek his forgiveness. And maybe your new demeanor will encourage all those so-called first-class Christians to do the same.

> *Lord, help me remember that you don't rank believers into different classes according to their past. Just as sin puts us all on the same level, your forgiveness lifts each one of us to a higher plane.*

Speaking of Elephants

What's the best thing to do when nobody's talking about the elephant in the room? Talk about the elephant in the room. If we keep ignoring it, it's like shooting ourselves in the foot. For the sake of keeping peace, we don't mention the obvious issue that everyone knows about, but no one will address out loud. We may think we're keeping the peace that way, but in reality we're just staying stuck. Our silence is contributing to the problem.

Here's an example: when a child's parent in the other home has an addiction or behavior problem and you avoid the subject. Sure it's hard, but you need to talk about it, speaking with respect and compassion for the involved parties, of course. Help your kids understand what's going on. Do your best to give them a godly perspective of how they can react to the situation, maybe even how they can help.

Awkward? For sure. But necessary in order to bring truth to the situation? Absolutely.

Lord, reveal to me any difficult issues I've been ignoring. Help me break the ice and begin talking about what our family most needs to discuss.

Steal a Kiss

One way to keep oxygen flowing to your marriage is to steal a kiss. Well, actually you're not really stealing it; you're drawing on your own bank account of affection. What you *are* stealing is a moment. A moment out of a hectic day, away from stress. A moment to step aside from the parenting role and remember the special bond you share as husband and wife.

Ironically, this type of stealing is also a way of giving. You see, a kiss is a much-needed point of connection. Research shows that when you have intimate moments built into your day, you oxygenate your marriage. Habits like a warm hug before work, a funny text exchanged, or a shared recreational activity help sustain your marriage in the midst of life's pressures.

So your mission for today: Find your moment and steal a kiss. As you do, you'll breathe new life into your marriage relationship. And that leads to a healthier family for everyone involved.

Loving Father, help me never to be too busy or grow too complacent to give my marriage the high priority it deserves. Teach me the best ways to make my beloved feel valued and cherished.

Celebrating Oneness

How do you celebrate marital oneness when your family isn't one? There may be a lot of people wondering about this on Valentine's Day. After all, this is a day to celebrate romance and love. But while you and your spouse may be doing well, there might be strife in your extended family with an in-law. Or maybe your blended family isn't so blended yet; you two are doing great, but you have concerns for the kids or stress between homes.

If you're in this situation, how are you supposed to enjoy a holiday like this? Well, you may have to compartmentalize a little bit. Just because *everything* is not hunky-dory doesn't mean that it's not okay to thank God for your spouse and celebrate what's going well in your marriage. During times of struggles, it's even more important to acknowledge the good in your life. There's no reason to feel guilty. Because if you wait to celebrate Valentine's Day until all your family relationships are perfect, you won't celebrate it until you get to heaven.

Today I choose to celebrate the blessings of my marriage by expressing love and appreciation to my spouse.

The Dance of Want

Are you dancing "the dance of want"? Remember when you were younger and got a crush on someone, but you didn't know if they were interested in you? So you acted coy. Before sticking your neck out, you tried to find out if they wanted to be wanted by you. That's the dance of want.

The first date turned out great and you hoped for another one, but you couldn't help wondering if they felt the same way. After dating for months you were thinking of marriage—but were they? The dance continued. Now you're married, but sometimes you wonder why you want conversation or sex more than they do.

Here's the deal: The dance can make you stand back and wait for proof that the other person wants you as much as you want them. But that gets you nowhere. So go ahead and love first. Give first. Sacrifice first. Want first—just like Christ did (and does) on behalf of you.

Father, you tell us in 1 John 4:19 that we love because you first loved us. Fill me with your Spirit so I can follow your example and not be afraid to reach out first.

A Balancing Act

Here's a more important question than the one about the chicken and the egg: Which comes first in your household—your marriage or the kids? Well, since prioritizing your marriage is what makes leading your children possible, the correct answer is actually *both*. Healthy stepcouples know that they must balance their time and energy to invest in their marriage and also in the lives of the children.

For example, because the transition to a stepfamily can make kids feel pushed aside, smart biological parents schedule time to connect one-on-one with their kids. But they also carve out a date night with their spouse. If the kids object to this, they patiently reassure them and then go on with the date.

Finding the right balance is not always easy, especially with today's busy pace and all the demands on our time. But those efforts sure pay off in the long run as you watch your marriage *and* your children flourishing.

Heavenly Father, help me order my days to focus the time and attention needed to nurture relationships with my spouse and with each one of my children.

A Smooth Transition

Moving between homes can be extremely stressful for kids. One way you can help is to make the transition as smooth and drama-free as possible. You see, when the transition is carried out in a positive and upbeat manner, kids feel safe to be themselves. They don't feel as though they are pawns being shoved back and forth by warring nations.

"I try to have a good attitude," said Cindy, "but I can't help coming unglued if my ex-husband looks at me wrong." And therein lies part of the problem. Cindy has made the between-home transition about *her* instead of about her children. She stays on edge. She dwells on the past before seeing her ex-husband. And she takes even his facial expressions personally. It's good that Cindy is aware of her vulnerability, but she has to grow beyond it for the sake of her kids.

Remember that you can make times of transition smoother for your children by making it about them, not about you.

Dear Lord, during times of transition take my focus off myself, and help me turn it toward the comfort and well-being of my children.

Connect the Dots

S ince parenting is rewarding but challenging at times, here's a discipline tip for parents and stepparents: Make sure to connect the dots. It's important to help children relate their choices or behavior to the consequences that follow. We help them do this when we assign age-appropriate responsibilities and then use fitting discipline when they fail to carry those out.

For example, if a child aged two or older spills their milk, they should clean it up. (Younger kids will need a little help.) If kids agree to finish their chores before supper but don't, they shouldn't get to eat until they do finish them. If they stay out past their curfew, they should be docked double the time next time, or not allowed to go out at all.

It's really not that difficult. And screaming is not required—or recommended. Just a firm, loving follow-through that helps them connect the dots. After all, doesn't God do this with us? Your kids will learn, just like you're learning.

Father, teach me to parent my kids in ways that help them learn the connection between choices they make and the natural consequences that follow.

Not Quite Ready to Join the Party

Are your kids invested in the success of your marriage? One of the sobering differences between first families and stepfamilies is that kids in stepfamilies are not always invested in the success of their parent's remarriage. Children from biological families are naturally committed to their parents' marital happiness. But children in stepfamilies are initially devoted to their parent, and not necessarily the new marital relationship.

It's vital for parents and stepparents to recognize this and not be surprised by a child's lack of encouragement. For example, if you don't get an anniversary card from your older kids the first few years, don't make a big deal out of it. Go ahead and celebrate your marriage. Just don't expect your kids to join you. And don't be tempted to lay a guilt trip on them because of their lack of enthusiasm. Because with time, they just might be ready to join the party.

Give me grace to handle my disappointment when my children don't show as much enthusiasm for my current marital relationship as my first. Help me be understanding and patient, looking forward to the day when they value it as much as I do.

An Endless Supply

Here's one major difference between biological families and blended families: In stepfamilies, relationships between family members often compete with rather than support each other. In a biological family, a parent who gives time and care to their child is also caring for their spouse at the same time. But in stepfamilies, time and energy given to one person often feels like a threat to someone else. For example, a stepparent may resent the time their spouse gives to their children. And children can feel jealous of the time their parent gives to the stepparent.

The basic issue here is insecurity. New relationships tend to feel like an invasion of old ones. To avoid a sense of competition, remind yourself that God provides us with an endless amount of love. You have more than enough love for every single person in your life—and they have more than enough love for you, too. As long as we let God be the source, we never need to worry about running out.

Father, you are the source of love. Thank you for allowing me to be a channel through which that love flows over each family member.

Connected by Grace

No matter how you're connected to a stepfamily—whether you're a grandparent, a stepsibling, a stepparent, or just a step-uncle-in-law—I want you to remember this: Grace connects, but possessiveness divides.

You know, the essential story of a stepfamily is *someone leaving* and *someone joining* a family. And whenever this happens, even under the best of circumstances, parents and kids feel some degree of insecurity. Unfortunately, that insecurity tempts us to become possessive—to pull some people toward us and to push others away. But our jealousy and possessiveness create division and conflict among family members. They also promote resentment toward *us*.

What brings peace is a spirit of grace, especially toward people we don't know very well. Stepchildren to stepparents, stepsibling to stepsibling, former wife to new wife.

So remember the grace that God has lavished on you, then turn around and freely offer it to others.

> *Remove any spirit of possessiveness from our family. Help us be grace-filled in all our interactions with each other.*

Faith, Hope, and Love

Many people cite 1 Corinthians 13 as one of their favorite Bible passages. Beyond the beautiful language used in this chapter, there's just something special about the concept of faith, hope, and love, isn't there? Over the centuries, philosophers like Aristotle have touted a list of virtues that they say promote human flourishing. But the Bible identifies these three. So how is God's list different?

Well, while the classical virtues of Aristotle promote the individual and the would-be hero, faith, hope, and love make you look away from yourself. They turn your eyes toward God and others. You become less self-centered, not more so.

In your home, is your faith in *yourself*? Do you hope in *your* ability to get it right? Do you demand love and attention from others? If so, turn your gaze up and out. Put your faith and hope in God and love him and your family with your whole heart. Because that's how we all truly flourish.

Father, help us live each day with faith in your character, hope in your promises, and hearts filled with love for you and for each other.

Feed Your Family

Have you ever noticed that in order to stay alive, you have to keep feeding yourself?

Obviously, you already knew that. That's a fact you can hardly forget; after all, if you're not feeding yourself, your stomach will remind you to get on with it. Well, relationships also need to be fed on a regular basis, or something—usually conflict—will remind you of that need.

One of the best foods to feed your relationships is appreciation. If you want to win or keep someone's heart, shower them with genuine compliments and don't stop. By contrast, be cautious about using criticism. Words of affirmation and appreciation can build up a stepfamily relationship, foster safety and closeness in a marriage, and even encourage cooperation between co-parents. But criticism can undo it all and build walls of resentment.

So don't just keep your family alive—help it thrive! Make sure to provide a steady diet of wholesome "food" that builds them up.

Holy Spirit, fill my mouth with words that infuse our home with
a spirit of acceptance and gratitude for each other.

God Will Make a Way

Ron, we are struggling and I just need a dose of encouragement."
Jon explained that he and his wife of two years had struggled with many of the challenges addressed in my books and DVDs. He added: "Specifically, we deal with my ex-wife's manipulation for more money. And my wife's ex-husband has anger issues. Plus, our five kids have us chasing our tails. We pray together every day, read meditations, and go to church, but still sometimes feel tempted to divorce."

Let's face it—it's hard to stay encouraged when there's no end in sight to our problems. That must have been how the Israelites felt when they ended up trapped between the Red Sea and Pharaoh's army. They had obeyed God's leading; now they faced certain death.

But God made a way by parting the waters for them to walk through. How could they have foreseen that? He will make a way for your family as well. Even if you can't see any way forward, don't quit. Keep walking in faith and trust him to open up a path.

Father, strengthen our faith as we allow you to guide us through our problems and conflicts.

Four Levels of Love

Nearly a thousand years ago French abbot Bernard of Clairvaux said there are four levels of love:

First, to love myself solely. (That's not love, that's just being self-absorbed.)

Second, to love you for my sake. (That's using people for personal gain. Know anybody like that?)

Third, to love you for your sake. (Now, that's more like it—selflessness.)

But the highest level of love, he said, is to love myself for your sake.[3] The idea of loving ourselves makes us uncomfortable, but notice the purpose of recognizing your worth (what he calls loving myself): loving others. Jesus made this same connection when he said to love your neighbor—*as yourself* (Matthew 19:19). Knowing you are valuable so you can give yourself away for the well-being of others is the highest form of love. And a great way to be a friend, spouse, parent, or child.

Lord, help me love and care for myself in such a way that I have even more to offer others and can better serve my family.

Good News about Your Marriage

Did you know that being optimistic about the future of your marriage actually improves your marriage? The widespread belief that half of all marriages end in divorce has led to a generation of frightened singles and young couples. But it turns out the actual divorce rate is much lower for first and blended family marriages than most people believe. So their fear is actually based on a myth.[4]

The best thing you can do is dial down your intimidation and worry. Living in fear of being a statistic leads couples to do things that make their marriage more vulnerable. In other words, being optimistic about your marital future frees you to laugh and love in ways that improve your relationship. So don't buy the lie. Live with confidence and trust God to teach you along the way.

Lord, we look to the future of our marriage with confidence, believing that you will teach us how to safeguard our relationship and make it the best it can be.

Marrying the Ex-Wife-in-Law

Meddling mother-in-law? What if you have a meddling ex-wife-in-law?

Nicole never saw it coming. While dating Tom she never anticipated how intrusive his ex-wife, Sharon, would be. Yes, on occasion, Sharon would send late-night texts or show up at Tom's front door unannounced, but Nicole assumed this would end once she and Tom married.

Nicole was wrong. In fact, as soon as they got married, things got worse. Okay, yes, it was unrealistic of Nicole to assume that Sharon would play nicely after the wedding, but no one could have predicted that Sharon would become more problematic and disrespectful. The point is this: to marry a divorced person is to gain a mother-in-law, a father-in-law, *and* an ex-spouse-in-law. Expect it. And accept it. Then work diligently with your spouse not to let the difficult ex-partner divide your marriage. You may not be able to stop their meddling, but you can determine how you deal with it together.

Father, help us deal with difficult family members with tact, respect, and Christlike love, always remembering that our marital relationship takes priority over all others.

Choose Faith over Fear

Have you ever noticed that fear pushes us to try to seize control? I certainly have noticed that in my life; maybe you have, too. We worry about our children so we pile on the guilt and manipulate them into making different choices. We feel afraid that our spouse doesn't really love us as much as we want, so we criticize them, hoping that will motivate them to love us more. And we argue with God over our circumstances so he will fix them according to our desires. How's that been working out for you?

Psalm 46:10 says, "Be still, and know that I am God." A simple command, but not always easy to follow. What would happen if we reacted differently when we worried or felt frightened? Instead of letting fear turn us into control freaks, what if we chose faith instead? The kind of faith that helps us give up control and trust God more deeply. Take a moment to imagine what that would look like in your life.

God, when I'm tempted to worry or feel afraid, still my heart and help me release control of my family and my life into your capable hands.

Cross-Cultural Kids

Did you know that most children of divorce are citizens of two countries, sort of? Even if you've never traveled outside the United States, you know that other countries have different social customs, holidays, religious practices, and often a different language. For children alternating between Mom's house and Dad's house, it can be like living in two countries. There may be different family rules, chores, and punishments. A totally different atmosphere.

I've always been amazed at how kids manage to adapt to these different cultures every other weekend. Sure, sometimes they need a gentle reminder—"You go to bed at 9:00 at our house, remember?" But generally, they adjust pretty well. Especially when both homes do their best to respect the preferences of the other home and don't make kids feel guilty for how things are done.

Your kids have dual citizenship in two countries; they belong in both. As ambassador of your home, do your part to foster peace between the two—for your kids' sake.

Help me maintain a respectful attitude about how things are done differently in my child's other home.

It's Not Real Until It's Real

R on, we dated for two years and everything seemed great with my kids. But the day we married, out of nowhere they changed their tune."

I hate to say it, but that's a common story I hear from couples in blended families. They're confused and baffled. And they often wonder what signs they missed before the wedding.

Let me quickly point out that kids are confused, too. They really did like the idea of the new family, and maybe they even felt drawn to the step-parent at some point. But the truth is, it's not real until it's real. Kids can't always anticipate how sad they're going to feel at the wedding or how displaced they'll feel afterward. Or the negative emotions that might erupt inside them. It has to become real for all of that to come to the surface.

And that's when adults need lots of patience—more patience than they've ever exercised before.

Loving Father, we ask you to give us supernatural patience as we deal with the confusion and negative emotions that unexpectedly surface during times of family changes.

Do What You Can Do

S uccess is never final. Failure is never fatal. It's courage that counts."[5]
Those are words quoted by Coach John Wooden, who won ten
NCAA national basketball championships over a twelve-year pe-
riod. He also said, "Do not let what you cannot do interfere with what
you can do."

That's a message I want my kids to get. I want them to understand that
while they can't do everything, they can make the most of their unique
God-given gifts. I'd also pray those words over stepparents who can't force
a stepchild's openness, over biological parents who can't make everyone
in their family happy, and over stepchildren who wish that divorce or
death had never happened.

There are many things in life that we can't do anything about, no matter
how much we wish otherwise. But what we *can* do is be patient, grace-
filled, and courageous to face today with love.

*Lord, show me what I can do right now to nurture each member
of my family, helping them discover and embrace your special
plan for their lives.*

Long-Distance Parents

How do you pull off long-distance parenting? There are a lot of parents who are physically distant from their children but want to remain engaged and active in their kids' lives. How can they manage that? I have a few suggestions.

First, develop some routines that keep communication alive. You might send a text on Monday, make a video-call on Tuesday, drop an Instagram on Thursday, and show up on Friday for your weekend visitation. And make sure to plan something special on birthdays and holidays.

To remind your kids of your presence, take lots of pictures and videos and make sure they have a copy so they can remember the good times. Look through the photos together occasionally.

And finally, when you do have time together, get out of the house. Get away from the TV, the computer, and video games. Take a walk together, play a game, run errands—whatever it takes to make the most of your time.

Father God, no matter how busy I am, strengthen my commitment to stay personally connected with each one of my children, whether they live in my home or in someone else's.

A Line in the Sand

Here's an enigma: How do you find permanence in a relationship without making a permanent commitment? In cohabitation that's what many people in our culture try to do. You know what a wedding represents? It's the day two people draw a line in the sand and together step over it—from singleness to a permanent relationship. I've heard some people argue that living with someone is essentially the same thing—that a piece of paper won't make any difference.

"Oh," I respond, "so it won't matter if you go ahead and get married." After which they start backpedaling pretty fast because deep down people intuitively know marriage is different; that's why they didn't step over that line in the first place. Paper may not make a difference, but commitment sure does.

You see, permanence in marriage focuses our choices toward the success of the relationship. Choosing cohabitation does not.

Father, every day help me renew my commitment to my spouse and children. Show me how to make choices that contribute to the health and well-being of our family.

Be Willing to Hear the Truth

In your family, are you free to speak the truth?

A good friend will tell you the truth. The truth about your clothes, about your behavior, about the impression you're giving off—the truth about . . . YOU. But sometimes families are afraid of hurting one another, so they don't grant each other permission to share honest opinions about such things.

But other than God, these people know you better than anyone else. And they're supposed to be your best friends, helping you become more Christlike. Who better to speak the hard truths that you need to hear?

Now answer this question: Have you given them permission to gently point out sin in your life? (Ouch.) Not in a critical or condemning way, but compassionately, just because they love you. Sure, it can be an awkward moment, but when done gently for your own good, why would you turn it down? So how about it? Does your family have your permission?

Lord, help our family create an atmosphere where each member feels free to speak—and hear—hard truths that will push us to grow more like you.

Grafted Together by Love

You know what a hybrid is, right? It's when two things are combined. When Mathew spoke at his stepmother's—or should I say, *mother's*—funeral, he talked about being grafted into her life by love. He said, "While we have no common blood and no matching physical characteristics, we have been grafted together by God as mother and son. I think sociologists would define us as a blended family. I prefer to think of us as a hybrid family, grafted together by God."[6]

When you graft two plants together it's a cool science experiment. When you graft two families together, the cutting and grafting process can be painful, but the end result is life-giving. Keep watering and feeding your hybrid blended family—and watch God grow it into something beautiful.

Lord God, thank you for grafting us into your family. Please watch over the growing process of our hybrid family, helping us move past the painful stages to reach full maturity and produce fruit that honors you.

The Parental Unity Rules, Part 1

P arenting was meant to be a team sport. Part of your strength in parenting comes from the unity between you and your spouse. So whether you're a stepfamily couple or a single parent relying on extended family for support, here's the first rule to maintaining your unity: Be proactive. Don't wait until problems occur to discuss your behavioral expectations, discipline techniques, or overall strategy for building character in your kids. You need to proactively plan how you will parent.

That sounds like a no-brainer, but you'd be surprised at how many couples parent on the fly without coordinating their efforts. About half of stepfamily couples get married without agreeing on a parenting strategy.[7] Look, you have to work hard to get on the same parenting page—and it's important that you do so. United you stand, but divided *they* fall.

Father, help us set aside time to pray together and discuss our kids' needs as we design a plan for parenting them that will bless and strengthen our family.

The Parental Unity Rules, Part 2

Now here's another no-brainer about blended families: Adding a stepparent to the parenting team is bound to change something. Yes, things will undoubtedly change. So here's another tip for maintaining parental unity when they do: Let the biological parent communicate any change in rules. Early on, in particular, a stepparent's authority will naturally be questioned. And when kids have certain expectations, ultimately they need to hear from their mom or dad. So you might as well begin there.

Have a parent meeting to discuss what the new rule is and how you're going to communicate it. Then stand side by side as the biological parent does much of the talking. If the kids blame the stepparent, the biological parent should make it clear that they themselves fully support the change. It's vitally important that you maintain a united front. Remember, united you stand, but divided *they* fall.

Give us wisdom and sensitivity as we adjust rules or set new ones, always showing the kids a united front as we explain necessary changes.

The Parental Unity Rules, Part 3

It's absolutely essential that parents work together. So here's another tip for maintaining parental unity. There are a lot of different ways to handle parenting decisions. Being able to support one another in those decisions is important. So when in doubt, call a parental meeting to get on the same page. It never hurts to say to a child, "Hey, let me get back to you on that," and then have a quick conversation with your spouse to dialogue about how you'd both like to handle the situation.

That brief discussion can maintain your harmony in parenting. Stepparents who are unsure of their role can really benefit from a check-in. And when a mom or dad takes time to check in with the stepparent, it speaks volumes to the children about their need to respect the stepparent, too. In parenting, never hesitate to go the extra mile. Because united you stand, but divided *they* fall.

Lord, help us demonstrate respect for each other and work to ensure harmony by checking in to share opinions on decisions regarding family matters.

The Parental Unity Rules, Part 4

Here's a tough question: How do you maintain parental unity when the two of you disagree? Nan and I have disagreed many times about how to most effectively parent our children. Even the most well-intentioned, good-hearted parents see things differently sometimes. But what do you do if one of you has already taken action?

Well, what you *don't* do is make critical comments in front of the kids about how the other handled something. Or even worse, you don't want to unilaterally reverse the decision. Either one of those actions seriously undercuts the other person's authority.

Instead, have a parent meeting behind closed doors and listen. Listen carefully. After all, maybe there's something you didn't know or fully understand about the situation. But then, if necessary, share your own thoughts about what might happen next time. Remember that parenting is a live-and-learn experience. Just as long as you live and learn . . . *together.*

When we disagree on how to handle a parenting issue, keep us willing to listen to each other's opinions and perspectives. And help us always present a unified front to our children.

Famous Stepkids

Time for a pop quiz: What do Ronald Reagan's and Bruce Willis's kids have in common?

Well, they have a stepparent. And so do Tom Brady's son, Halle Berry's daughter, Kirk Franklin's son, Will Smith's son, and the children of Kevin Costner and T.I. And how about Matt Damon, Megan Fox, Daniel Craig, Steven Spielberg, and the wife of Prince Charles, Camilla, the Duchess of Cornwall—what do they have in common? They're all stepparents.

What about famous stepchildren? Can you name any? It depends on your definition of famous, of course, but perhaps Hansel and Gretel, Cinderella, former President Barack Obama, Priscilla Presley, John Lennon, and Princess Diana would fit the category. And many Bible characters lived in a different sort of blended family due to the practice of polygamy: Isaac, Joseph, and Solomon just to name a few. Oh, and let's not forget Jesus, stepson to Joseph.

So, what's the point? Simply this: Not only are you not alone, you're in good company.

> *Lord, thank you for the reminder that we are surrounded by other stepfamilies who have been blessed in their new relationships. We don't ask for fame, but for your favor and grace.*

The Mom and Stepmom Alliance

Fairy tales often portray a mom and stepmom pitted against each other. But it's a wish come true for kids when they aren't. I just love it when people send me their success stories. For example, I heard from a stepmom who attended one of my stepfamily conferences and learned how to respond in a loving way to her husband's difficult ex-wife.

You see, the mom resented the stepmom and felt threatened by her. She talked bad about her and poisoned her kids' minds against their stepmom. But despite such unfair treatment, the stepmom responded in love and respect toward the mom. And with time, her goodwill won the mom over.

Together, they emailed me a picture of the two of them laughing and holding one another's children. And guess what? Exchanging kids for visitation is no longer a nightmare for the two families. Now that's a fairy tale every kid hopes will come true.

Father, thank you for promising that love will overcome evil. Help us respond to each member of our families with respect and Christlike love, even if they are hostile toward us.

The Dad and Stepdad Alliance

What happens when a dad and stepdad team up? Kids win—that's what happens.

Maybe you saw the story about the dad who paused before walking his daughter down the aisle at her wedding and said, "I'll be back." Then he bolted down the aisle, grabbed the arm of his daughter's stepdad, and said, "Come on! You helped raise her; now help me walk our daughter down the aisle."

Wow. After years of animosity and competition, he said "our daughter." I'm sure you can imagine what happened next. The daughter was crying, the stepdad was crying—everybody in the whole church was crying. And the bride's two dads walked her down the aisle.

Of course the story went viral and even made the national news. As well it should have. Because that kind of selflessness is how you truly bless a child. And maybe even change a nation.

Thank you, Lord, for examples like this that demonstrate what can happen when blended family members learn to love each other selflessly. Help our family rise above pettiness and jealousy to bless each other with that kind of sacrificial love.

The Good Thing about Disharmony

Some people think they've heard a few crazy-sounding suggestions come out of my mouth, but this one probably takes the cake: Learn to endure disharmony in your home. Before you panic, let me explain. I don't mean be okay with disharmony in your blending family. I don't expect you to be happy when someone is unhappy. What I am saying is that disharmony is a natural part of becoming a family.

When a wedding forms a stepfamily, you lack a family identity. People have different last names, different pets, traditions, bedtimes, expectations, parenting styles. . . . The list goes on and on. What you have to do is figure out how you're going to act like a family. That process practically guarantees a little disharmony—maybe even a lot!

Learn to take it in stride. Ironically, the struggle to figure life out produces respect, trust, and appreciation for each other. As you work through things you become family. But if you panic every time there's disharmony, you short-circuit the process. So take a deep breath, whisper a prayer, and keep going.

Give us patience as we work through this complicated process of becoming a family in the truest sense.

Love by Choice

One unique feature of stepfamily living is that it represents a chance to imitate God's choice to love. When you're born into a family, love is normally automatic. But think about it: In blended families people have to *choose* love. Stepparents choose to love children who are not their own. Stepsiblings make the decision to call each other brother and sister. And stepchildren, even if not formally adopted by their stepparent, get to be adopted by that stepparent's heart.

If this sounds familiar to you, maybe it reminds you of what the Bible teaches about our relationship with God. Romans 8, among other places, explains that God, our heavenly Father, has adopted us into his family. He certainly didn't have to, but he did. Just because he loves us so much.

Sounds to me like blended families get to be a living picture of God's choosing kind of love. How cool is that?

Loving Father, today I will follow your example. I choose to unconditionally love those in my family circle, not because I should or because I have to, but because of your love for all of us.

Proper Ventilation Required

Ever feel like you've just gotta scream? If you're co-parenting a child with someone who lives in a different home, you've probably heard how important it is that you speak respectfully about that parent in front of your kids. Critical remarks or open anger and bitterness put kids in the middle and hurt them; after all, that's their *parent* you're complaining about.

What do you do, though, with all the frustrating feelings you've got bottled up inside? You do need to vent, but make sure you do it in private. Find a trusted friend, support group, or counselor to help you process your emotions. You can talk to your spouse sometimes, but that just lays the frustration on them—and what are they supposed to do with it?

Bottom line: Find a good outlet, but never vent in front of your kids. And don't forget that the One who loves your family most is always ready to listen.

Lead me to the proper resources to help me handle my frustrations and negative emotions in healthy ways, always careful to protect my kids from being hurt by them.

Driving Away Ghosts

Now, here's a delicate situation: What do you say to your spouse when you see a haunting in progress? No, I'm not talking about a real ghost. I'm talking about the negative memories or experiences from our past that haunt us. Let's be honest—we all have something that lingers in the background of our mind. A feeling that we're not good enough. Or the fear that someone who says they love us today won't be around tomorrow.

So what do you do when you see your spouse's past interfering with your present relationship? First, remember that your mate needs gentleness and understanding, not criticism or judgment. Then, with great compassion you might say, "Something tells me this is harder for you than I realize. I'm wondering if you've ever felt this before?" Then pause and listen . . . and love.

The best way to drive away dark shadows from a hurtful past is to bring them into the light.

Give us the courage to honestly share our past hurts so that instead of weakening our relationship, they serve to strengthen our marriage.

Money: Handle with Care

Want to know a surefire way to start a fight in a stepfamily? Just start talking about money. You know, financial matters really bring out the best and the worst of our character. In stepfamilies, sometimes the discussion reveals differing emotional connections and loyalty issues between family members. If not handled carefully, the topic of money can be used as a weapon to divide.

I often hear from stepparents who feel pushed out when their adult stepson asks their parent to add their name to the checking account or on the life insurance policy. Then there are the cases of those who discover that their spouse has been lending money to a child without their knowledge or consent.

In blended families, there's no room for secrets or emotional games, especially between spouses. The way you handle money should draw you together, not push you apart.

Lord, grant us wisdom to handle our finances in ways that draw us closer as a couple, making decisions together as partners and never having financial secrets from each other.

Guard against Jealousy

C an you imagine telling a parent to abandon their own child? No, you probably can't. But that's exactly what this stepmom said—to her own husband about his firstborn son. I guess she felt worried that her son would be short-changed in the family will. She told her husband in no uncertain terms, "Get rid of him because he will never be an heir along with my son."

Now try to imagine how awful that situation must have been for the whole family. But that's exactly what Sarah said to Abraham about his son Ishmael, born through Sarah's Egyptian maid. And according to Genesis 21:11 (NASB), "The matter distressed Abraham greatly because of his son." (Yeah, you think?)

Okay, let's learn something from this. Jealousy and insecurity destroy family relationships. They divide, devour, and cause great distress. So pray to get rid of jealousy, and ask God for an open, gracious heart toward all family members. After all, through God's abundant provision, there is plenty of inheritance for everyone.

Dear Lord, please remove all traces of jealousy from our family.
Knit our hearts together as one.

In-Laws and "Out-Laws"

How do you refer to that woman who married into your family: "our daughter-in-law" or "our daughter"? Words have meaning. When parents talk about their daughter-in-law, they are talking about the woman their son married. She may be family now, but she's not related by blood. It works the other way, too. In-laws typically refer to their mother-in-law as just that—not as their mom.

Then again, in some families, the relationship between in-laws is so strong that they do call each other Daughter or Mom. It just depends. The same thing is true in stepfamilies. A dad might say to his kids, "Mom texted and dinner's in the oven" even when "Mom" is a stepmom to one of the kids. They know what he means.

Yes, it will probably feel awkward at first, and you may have to explain sometimes. But that's the secret: Keep talking and defining your terms. Eventually, the outsiders will just become family.

Help us learn to use words and terms that affirm our family relationships, regardless of how awkward they seem at first.

Let the Child Set the Pace

Want to know the cardinal rule for building a strong relationship with a stepchild? It's pretty simple: Let the child set the pace. Allowing them to set the pace means gauging their level of openness to you and then matching it in kind.

If they pursue physical affection from you, don't leave them wanting. However, if they bristle when you try to hug them, back off a bit. Find something less intimidating. If they call you Daddy or Mommy, by all means, let them! But if they would prefer to call you by your first name, that's okay, too.

If they seek out time with you, get out and do something together. But if they keep their distance, find one thing you share in common and leave it at that. Just remember, letting them set the pace is how you start building the relationship. Then trust that it will grow over time.

Father, give me the patience to let my stepchild set the pace in our relationship and the discernment I need to guide my behavior.

Drop Some Weight

Want to discover a diet that is sure to take some weight off? Learn how to honor God.

Now, we honor lots of things. We honor our fallen heroes, our father and mother, the requests of our superiors at work; and we have an "honor system" we hope will keep people honest.

So what does it mean to honor God? The Old Testament root word for *honor* means "heavy" or "weighty"; essentially it means to give weight to someone, to grant them respect or authority in your life. We're called to honor God above all things, including ourselves. So I guess you could say we honor God by dieting. First, take the weight off yourself, and then in humility, through worship and obedience, place it on him.

Now that's a diet every home needs. Maybe your body won't lose any pounds, but it's sure to take a load off your mind and make you feel lighter in spirit.

Every day let me learn to honor you above all else, God. Help me show my kids that I respect your authority over me, so they can respect my authority over them.

Skip the Guilt Trip

"Mom, you always let me go *before*! You're just saying no now because *he* wants you to."

Have you ever noticed that kids are really good at buying us tickets for a guilt trip? But then, guilt is one of a child's best tools for getting what they want. This technique can prove especially effective on parents who marry and bring a stepparent into their kids' lives—and now the rules are changing. The parent feels a little guilty about that, and the child learns how to capitalize on their guilt.

So what do you do? First, you and your spouse need to strive for unity as a parenting team at all costs. When a conflict pops up, admit to your child that yes, things *have* changed. But don't give in when you need to stand your ground. Instead, respond honestly with a positive note: "You're right. Some rules have changed and I'm sure that's confusing for you. But this is the new rule and I expect you to follow it. Love ya!"

As we sort out blended rules brought about by family changes, help us respond in a firm but positive manner to disagreements and complaints.

The Journey through Grief

C hildren grieve for lots of different reasons. Sometimes despite good intentions, our attitudes actually make things worse for a hurting child. It's ironic—grief is an emotion that will not be denied. But in our culture, we sure do our best to deny it. We expect sad people to get over it in a few weeks. We act as though faith and a quick sermon from Romans 8:28 will make sadness go away. But it doesn't.

What kids need is not denial, but caregivers who give them permission to be sad. They need someone willing to listen to their stories and then share their own struggles. Children need adults who will be authentic with their sadness—like Asaph, who cried out to the Lord in Psalm 77, and Jesus, who cried with his friends over the loss of Lazarus in John 11—so they can be authentic with theirs.

Grief is a journey, not a destination. And it's best for children not to travel that road alone.

During times of grieving keep me sensitive to my children's needs, always making myself available when they need to talk.

Check Your Progress

On any journey, part of gauging your progress is knowing how far you've come and how far you still have to go. Those who study productivity and team efficiency will tell you that you need to be able to measure your progress so you can know what you've accomplished.

I think parenting is like that. It's easy to identify qualities our children are missing and what we need to work on as a parent. But sometimes we fail to notice how far they've come or how our parenting skills have improved. Stepfamilies can start to feel like a never-ending work in progress. And that can be discouraging.

Why not take a minute and remember what it was like in the beginning of this blended adventure? Get some perspective on how far you've come—and celebrate that progress. And know that God is always with you, now and in all that still lies ahead.

God, when I feel discouraged, open my eyes to see the progress our family has made together. I know that we are a work in progress, and I trust your hand to guide us through.

Schedule a Business Meeting

Parents, it may be time for a business meeting. Without a doubt, lots of parenting and family decision-making takes place on the fly. We're pretty much making it up as we go along, aren't we? Well, that's exactly why we need to slow down and get proactive with a planned time to discuss what's going on with the kids. Call it a business meeting if you like, but you need to do it.

I recommend that co-parents, meaning divorced or divided parents, do the same thing. You can address schedules, report cards, behavior training, and spiritual development.

You don't discuss your personal life or bring up old issues that ignite angry feelings because this is a parental meeting, not a personal one. Drawing the line between those two is crucial.

But if you can do it, your kids win. And if you can't have a reasonable business meeting for your kids' sake, it's time to find a counselor who can help.

Father, help us be more purposeful and deliberate in our parenting, carving out time for focused discussions on family issues— and always looking to you as the CEO of our family.

Engaged to the Savior

Here's a reminder you won't hear at a marriage conference: There's no marriage in heaven. You might be thinking, *Gee, Ron, that's not very romantic.* I know. But that's what Jesus says in Matthew 22:30: "For in the resurrection they neither marry nor are given in marriage."

You see, as Christ's bride we're all engaged to the Savior. Marriage here on earth is meant to lead us to our ultimate wedding, if you will, where there won't be a need for marriage as we now know it. I suppose that means that even now, our love for Christ should far outweigh our earthly loves. Marriage should move us closer to Christ, not compete with him for our affection and attention.

Now, with that perspective in mind, how should you date? How should you love your spouse? Or prepare your children for marriage? Things change drastically when we think about relationships in light of eternity.

Lord Jesus, enlarge my idea of marriage and family relationships so that I can see others as you see them—from the perspective of eternity.

March 29

To Filter or Not to Filter

Is your family communication filtered or unfiltered? In this digital age we have a lot of communication filtering options. Say your mobile phone rings, but you don't want to talk to that person at the moment. So you choose to let it go to voice mail. Later, you can listen to the message and reply with a text if you want to. That's filtering.

Now, this ability has pros and cons. For blended families, there are times when filtering can be helpful to reduce conflict in strained relationships—say, between ex-spouses. But if new family members don't stop filtering at some point and put down the phone on occasion, you'll never develop an authentic relationship. Filtering can help in the beginning, but there's no depth in the communication until you actually talk—and hang out—in person.

Talking in person . . . now there's a throwback idea that needs a comeback.

Father, help me be attentive to the best moments to engage family members in deep, face-to-face conversation that draws us closer to each other.

The Joy Set before Him

Have you ever faced a great trial in your life—*with joy*? I remember a day when my wife and I walked into a room and met with doctors who told us that our twelve-year-old son was about to die. I can assure you, I did not face that moment with joy.

The writer of Hebrews says in the Bible to look to Jesus, "the founder and perfecter of our faith, who for the joy that was set before him endured the cross" (12:2). Where was the joy in enduring the cross?

In this Easter season, let's remember that Jesus looked past his suffering to the day when he would be glorified at his Father's side—and when the path for you and for me to join him would be complete. His joy is in having you near. All the more reason to worship and praise him.

Lord Jesus, during times of trials and suffering help us remember the example you set as you faced the cross. May our grief and sorrow be tempered by the promise that our joy-filled future with you makes any earthly hardship pale in comparison.

A Reason to Hunt for Eggs

Ever wonder why many people consider searching for eggs a great way to celebrate Christ's resurrection? Does it seem to you like there's a little disconnect there? If you've studied the history of early Christianity, you probably know that at some point the egg became a symbol of the tomb of Jesus. The outer shell hides the fact that there is life going on inside. And just as a bird eventually emerges from an egg, Jesus rose from the dead and broke out of the tomb.

So on Easter weekend, why not color some eggs and have a hunt? But make sure the kids understand the reason behind this fun tradition. Explain to them about the resurrection power of Christ that is available to help us overcome our own tomb of sin and imperfection.

In John 11:25 Jesus said, "I am the resurrection and the life. Whoever believes in me, though he die, yet shall he live." Besides those colored eggs, help your children find the ultimate hope available through Jesus.

Father, as we prepare our hearts to celebrate your resurrection, help us use our holiday traditions as teaching moments to nurture our children's faith.

He's Alive!

ave you forgotten to rejoice?

Peter and John must have been thinking all kinds of wild thoughts as they ran toward the tomb that Sunday morning. Mary Magdalene had told them it was empty, and that Jesus had gone. Empty? Gone? Gone where? How—and why?

John 20:1–20 tells us that after Peter and John examined the strips of linen and the burial cloth that had been wrapped around Jesus, they believed. But it wasn't until later that evening when Jesus appeared to them in person that they rejoiced. And oh, how they must have rejoiced.

So what about us? We've heard the story of Christ's resurrection so many times that we may have become dulled to its wonder. Or maybe we've never really understood what it means. Even if we do believe, do we still rejoice over it?

Haven't you heard the news? The tomb is empty! And we serve a risen Savior!

Lord Jesus, fill us today with a renewed sense of wonder and awe at the meaning of the empty tomb. And fill our lives with your resurrection power as we serve you and each other.

Learn Obedience

Hebrews 5:8 tells us that Jesus *learned* obedience. Does that sound surprising? Well, when the writer of Hebrews said that Jesus "learned obedience through what he suffered," he wasn't suggesting that Jesus had been disobedient before. He was explaining that Jesus, who was already obedient to the Father's will, gained a deeper understanding of the value of obedience through practicing it when he was tempted. Practicing obedience during suffering made his understanding more perfect.

Now, it seems to me that marriage, parenting, and family relationships allow us plenty of chances to practice obedience, especially when we're tempted not to. We can choose to forgive when we've been hurt, to be self-controlled when we're disappointed, to be patient and gentle when worried, and to love even when we are being taken for granted. As we follow Jesus' example and practice obedience, we will mature in our understanding.

Father, today I choose to practice obedience to your instructions and your will, even when I don't feel like doing it or when I don't understand why I should set aside my personal rights. I will imitate Jesus and learn the value of obeying you.

High Stress Level

Here's a fun fact for you: In the early years of a blended family, the level of stress is typically very high. Well, of course, that's not fun at all. And it makes some people question whether they made a mistake—which just makes things even harder for everyone involved.

Remind yourself that stress is normally high for stepfamilies in the beginning, *and it does not mean that you made a mistake*. Merging traditions, parenting styles, personal preferences, backgrounds, family rules, and more is just plain tough. And not everyone in the house is going to be happy with everything that is taking place.

Listen, your family is in process, and that's okay. Remember that the mood today does not predict tomorrow. Over time as you figure out some things, the stress will come down and your family harmony will go up. And so will your fun factor.

Father, help me remember that stress is a natural part of the blending process and not a sign that our family is a mistake.

Start a Ministry

All over the world couples are starting marriage education groups, and churches are hosting events using resources from me and other ministry leaders.[8] Roger called to say, "I'm not a trained pastor. But you were right—with the resources you provided, my wife and I started a small group for stepfamily couples in our home, and it's working! Everyone loves the community and study—and lives are being changed."

It's amazing how one ordinary couple plus a practical resource can equal changed lives for God's glory. Sadly, few churches currently have a blended family ministry. And while more churches are catching the vision for how they can support stepcouples, most lack the leadership to even begin.

Maybe God is calling you to launch a ministry. It might be a few couples who meet in your living room or a Sunday school class—just get started and watch the ministry come alive! Use a resource that will teach the lesson while you facilitate the conversation. With God's help, you can do it. And you will see lives changed.

Lord God, use us to support and encourage other stepfamilies.
We trust you enough to follow wherever that leads us.

"I Don't Have to Do What You Say!"

What does a stepdad say when his stepdaughter declares, "You're not my dad; I don't have to do what you say"? Sometimes kids defy a stepparent's authority because they are hurting. True, she doesn't want to clean up her room, but she also misses her dad. A wise stepparent responds with compassion: "You're right, I'm not your dad. And I can tell you miss him." This connects with the child's heart and shows them that you're not all bad. In fact, your gentleness just might earn you some respect.

You also have to deal with the behavioral issue of the moment: "But I am the adult here right now, and you still have to clean your room. Besides, if your mom were here she'd be asking you to clean your room, too. It's your call; you can clean it yourself or we'll use your allowance to pay your sister to do it for you." Then turn and walk away.

Kids need understanding. They also need to clean their rooms.

Help me discipline my children with the right combination of firmness and gentleness, always respecting their feelings as I teach them to respect my authority.

Same Family, Different Viewpoints

Ron, I finally figured it out. I live in a stepfamily, but my husband doesn't."

As I talked with this stepmom, she revealed that she had just had an epiphany. As a stepmom of four, she frequently felt like an outsider and complained about it. But her husband just couldn't see things from her perspective. Then one day it dawned on her: "He *can't* experience the family the way I do. He is an insider with everyone; I'm the only outsider."

So what can you do in a situation like this? Don't blame your stepfamily experience on each other. That just pushes you apart. Recognize that the other person has a legitimate perspective—and be willing to be influenced by it. In this case, the husband can start listening to his daughters through his wife's ears, and the wife can stop expecting him to feel her every frustration. Always remember: Your mate is not your enemy.

Father, keep me aware that my relationship with our family is different from my spouse's perspective. Give us understanding of each other's views so we can work together for the good of everyone.

The Fear Factor

What if I told you that couples in blended families have a particular vulnerability that husbands and wives in first marriages don't have. Would you care to know what it is? Research reveals that couples in stepfamilies have an Achilles heel that undercuts their ability to love and trust. For someone who has already been through one divorce, the fear of another one—or worrying that your spouse isn't committed to you—predicts with 93 percent accuracy whether you have a strong, stable marriage or a fragile, unhappy one.[9]

Proverbs 6 tells us that jealousy arouses anger (v. 34). And jealousy is exactly what happens when fear and worry have their way. If you're in a blended family, it's essential that you find ways of casting out all fear; otherwise that fear may result in a self-fulfilling prophecy.

Loving Father, help us learn to obey 1 Peter 5:7, casting all our cares and anxieties on you. Help us look toward our future together with confidence and trust in you and in each other.

For Kids:
Coping with Loss

Parents, for the next five days you'll be reading devos designed for your kids that will also be helpful to you. Sharing them with your children will likely spark important conversations. Read each first and then decide whether to share. By the way, it's no mistake this series comes near Easter. We all have "Friday" seasons of death and darkness, but there is reason to hope, for Sunday is just around the corner.

Today I'm talking to kids (of all ages)—and the adults who love them. For the next few days I want to acknowledge some of the tough things you may be facing. Loss and sadness might be at the top of that list. Maybe life has thrown you some curves. Like not having your parents together, or losing one of them to death. Or having to move between homes, which causes problems like forgetting your math book at the other house. Not to mention adjusting to a stepparent whom you may not have asked for.

Here's what you need to know: God cares. He gets it. He hasn't forgotten you. And he will see you through, just as he did the many Bible characters who experienced great loss. You can trust him.

Take a minute now to talk to God about one of your most troubling losses.

For Kids: Wrestling with Guilt

Tracy knows in her head that she didn't cause her parents' divorce, but in her heart she believes she had something to do with it. She can't help feeling as though it's her fault somehow. Worst of all, she doesn't feel like she can talk to anybody about her guilt.

Every time Juan's dad invites him over *on his mom's weekend,* he finds himself in a tug-of-war, as though he has to choose between them. His parents have no idea how much he struggles with this. He even acts like he didn't enjoy himself so the other parent won't feel left out. Of course, this comes at a great price: He can't be happy and relaxed at either home.

Hey, Tracy and Juan, you're just kids. Taking care of your parents is not your responsibility. Please release that burden of guilt. Ask God to take the weight off your shoulders. And then go and enjoy the good things about your family—or families.

Ask God now to take away any unnecessary guilt and to help you tell your parents when you feel stuck between them.

For Kids: I'm Confused

Kids, have you ever felt happy and sad about your family, all at the same time? Or maybe sometimes you like your stepparent, but in that same moment you find yourself wanting to push back away from them. Yeah, I know it's confusing. I understand that there are some good things about your family, and also a few things that you would change in a heartbeat if it were up to you.

So first, how can you deal with all the confusing emotions? Accept them. Give yourself permission to feel all of them. Then make the choice to live with the situation and to make the best of it. This doesn't mean you're thrilled about everything that's happened in your family; it just means you're finding a way to cope.

With God's help, you can do more than cope—you can enjoy your life again. And don't worry, you won't always feel so confused.

Ask God right now to help you enjoy what is good about your family and wrestle through what is not so good.

For Kids: Face Your Fear

Any time we experience loss, it can make us become afraid of more loss. Two years into his mom's marriage, John, who is seventeen, told me, "I'm afraid of getting close to anyone. With all I've had to live through, I keep waiting for bad things to happen all over again." His fourteen-year-old brother Randy said, "I try to get closer to my stepdad sometimes, but then the fear happens. . . . I want to get close, but not too close."

Hey, I get it. You have good reason to hold back. You've been hurt. People have disappointed you. But here's the thing about fear: It paralyzes you and makes it hard to laugh and to love. Sometimes it makes you wonder if you'll ever feel normal again or enjoy life the way you used to.

Don't deny your fear—face it instead. Talk to God about it, knowing that he understands and wants to help you. And overcome that fear with something much better: love.

Ask God to help you take the risk of getting close to new people in your life by being kind to them and enjoying it when they are kind to you.

For Kids:
Share Your Sadness

Have you ever noticed that sometimes when we're sad inside, we act grumpy on the outside? Eighteen-year-old Rachel said that her mother and brother complained about how hard it was to get along with her lately. She didn't understand why they felt that way.

We soon figured out why. Her mom had started dating a guy, and that made her miss her father. He had died a few years before, and now she felt like she was losing him all over again. But instead of being sad and sharing her grief with her family, she reacted by being grumpy and cranky with everyone.

You know, when your heart hurts, the best way to deal with it is to actually be sad and not ignore the way you feel. Being grouchy just creates more problems for you and everybody else. So talk to someone you trust about your sadness. Be honest about it. Give your heart a chance to find comfort.

God, please help me to be sad instead of mad at people. Comfort me and help me control how I act toward others.

Good Reason
to Stick Together

Most couples divorce anyway, so if you're having problems, you might as well just accept the inevitable."

No, actually that's wrong. That attitude is based on the belief that half of all marriages end in divorce. And while we hear that statement tossed around a lot, it simply is not true. What's more, 80 percent of couples report that they're "somewhat to very" happy.[10]

If you don't fall into the happy category, let me encourage you to stick it out. Research clearly shows that couples who stay together during stressful times report five years later being very happy they did.[11] And stepfamily couples who stay married at least five years discover many rewards—just because they didn't quit.

Just—don't—give—up! In the long run, you and your children will be very glad you didn't.

Father, I pray that our commitment and devotion to each other sets an example that will bless our children's future relationships.

Be Quick to Forgive

Have you ever noticed how much easier it is to forgive a family member than someone else? I certainly have noticed this in my own life. I find it much harder to forgive an acquaintance compared to a close friend or family member. I suppose that's because my family is a part of me. Plus, I'm more deeply invested in my family relationships.

Sometimes stepparents and stepchildren find it more difficult to forgive each other than other family members. One teen said it this way, "If my dad hurts my feelings, it's a lot easier to let it go than if my stepmom does." Easier? Yes. But any more important? No.

In Ephesians 4:32, and many other passages, the Bible urges us to forgive our grievances with each other, just as God has forgiven us. And as best I can tell, that includes stepfamily members, too.

Father, thank you for forgiving my sins on the basis of the sacrifice Christ made on the cross. In light of that, help me be ready and willing to extend forgiveness to others who wrong me, without regard to closeness of relationship.

Don't Be a Threat

How do you convince stepchildren that you're not trying to take their parent's place? I'm sure you understand how all-important the answer to this question is, because a child who thinks you are trying to usurp their parent's rightful place will likely work their hardest to prevent you from doing so.

My advice is to just tell them, plain and simple, "I will never try to take your parent's place in your heart." And if the biological parent is still living, assure that parent, too. A stepmom might say to the mom: "Hey, I just want you to know that I know you're the mom, not me. I will always respect that and speak well of you to your children. My job is to bless your kids, not to get in the way."

Taking this approach lowers the child's and parent's threat level and their need to oppose the stepparent. It invites cooperation, not conflict. And as the threat level goes down, the peace and happiness level is sure to go up.

> *Heavenly Father, may my speech and my behavior always reflect a spirit of cooperation and respect for my stepkids' biological family members.*

Catch Them Doing Something Right

Okay, parents, get ready for the single best discipline strategy known to mankind, with a double bonus for stepparents. But first, let's admit how easy it is to notice disobedience and negative behavior. We spot that right away, but what we often miss is when children obey, follow through, or live out a virtue. The best way to shape a child's behavior is to notice them doing what you want and then draw attention to it. In other words, catch them doing something right.

Think about it—the same principle applies to adults as well. Compliments put a smile on *your* face and encourage *you,* right? Ephesians 4:29 urges us to build others up, "that it may give grace to those who hear." Well, children also benefit greatly when they know they've hit the mark. Sincere praise motivates them to continue the positive behavior.

And stepparents, when you compliment a stepchild, it has the added benefit of strengthening your relationship with the child. Double bonus!

Lord, help me spend less time noticing the negatives in my children's behavior and more time focusing on the positive aspects that deserve sincere praise.

Slow Down and Listen

R on, I'm marrying a man with adult children. Our transition should be easier since they're out of the house, right?"

Each year thousands of single people who have empty nests marry. A common assumption is that their adult children will be okay with it since they live on their own. But in reality adult stepfamilies have just as many adjustments to work through as younger stepfamilies. The issues vary, but the amount of work involved is about the same.

Of course, there are multiple sides to this story. The marrying couple hopes for their kids' blessing. The adult child complains that home just doesn't feel like home anymore. Biological parents feel caught between their new spouse and the kids, and the new spouse feels like an outsider who can't find their way into the family.

No matter which category you fit in, slow down a bit and listen to each other. Move past your assumptions and find out what the other needs from you. It might take a while, but growing together is worth it.

Help us keep realistic expectations during times of transition,
always ready to listen to all sides of our family story.

Give the Gift of Time

Sometimes the best way to build a bridge to your stepchild's heart is to stay away from them. I know that doesn't make a lot of sense—until you understand that one of the things kids in stepfamilies miss is time alone with their biological parent. Just think about how their world has changed. Since you came along they have to share their parent with you, and perhaps with your kids (if you have them).

So every once in a while, why not give your stepchildren exclusive time with their biological parent—your spouse—so they can once again feel the security of that relationship? You'll be offering them something they desperately need. And when they see that you're not competing with them for their parent's time and attention, they just might view you as a friend. Now, wouldn't that be nice?

Show us how to meet our children's needs so well that they always feel accepted, secure, and loved. As parents, help us make ourselves fully accessible and sensitive to those times when a child needs individual time with one of us.

Connect to Your Child's Heart

O ne of my goals is connecting you with your child's heart. The other day I had a conversation that warmed *my* heart. A dad had listened to a podcast where I talked about kids, divorce, and blended families. It got him wondering if his daughter felt the way I had described. So he asked her. And sure enough, she did. But there was more.

You see, before their conversation she didn't have words for what she was feeling. Oddly enough, in asking her if she felt a certain way, he gave words to her experience and helped her talk about it. But there was even more.

Before he initiated the conversation, she had felt disconnected from her father and unable to talk to him about awkward stepfamily issues. He hadn't known that. The conversation and her dad's listening ear made her feel close to him, not alone. Supported, not isolated. Loved, not forgotten. The combination of a quick question and an open heart turned into shared feelings and connected souls.

Father God, prompt me by your Spirit to ask questions that can initiate heart-to-heart conversations with my kids that draw us closer to each other.

Take Off, Put On: Introduction

Out with the old and in with the new. Sounds like a great idea, but where do we start? In Ephesians 4:22–24, the Bible calls Christians to put off the old self and to put on the new. I don't know about you, but for me that's really intimidating. A new righteous and holy self, one that rejects my natural human desires and instead imitates Christ's sacrificial lifestyle? How in the world do I manage that?

Paul tells us to be renewed in the spirit of our mind. So as a first step, try this: Write out a list of attitudes and behaviors you need to put off. I know, it's an ugly list, but you have to identify what you need to get rid of. Then review the fruit of the Spirit listed in Galatians 5:22–23. The goal is to renew your mind, put off the old, and put on the fruit. I'll give you some examples over the next few days, but get started with your list today.

Examine my heart, Lord, and show me which attitudes, habits, and behaviors are not pleasing to you.

Put On Forgiveness

In some ways discipleship is simply about putting off and putting on. One of the virtues God tells us to put on is forgiveness. Well, what do you have to put *off* in order to put forgiveness *on*? For starters, we need to get rid of the idea that forgiveness is condoning or excusing an offense; it's not that at all. It's not forgetting or denying the significance of it either—just the opposite, in fact. When someone wrongs us, forgiveness recognizes the full impact on us, but refuses to harbor a need for vengeance.

It's also putting off feeling weak when we've been hurt, or the belief that justice will no longer be found. No, forgiveness is empowering for a person who has been wronged. And while the offender still might have to pay a debt to society, you are releasing them from their debt to you. Just as God, in Christ, has forgiven your debt to him.

Lord Jesus, you gave us the ultimate example of forgiveness when you used some of your final breaths to pray for those who had crucified you. With your help, I commit to extending forgiveness to those who wrong me.

Put On Gentleness

When our boys were young, my wife gave me some feedback one day: "Ron, you are a great dad. But when you discipline our kids, you should see your face. You're intimidating, and I can tell the boys feel rejected." Well, that was hard for me to hear. But I took her words to heart. Her observation helped me understand that I needed to add the fruit of gentleness to my discipline techniques.

It wasn't easy, but it was definitely worth the effort. It turns out that being soft and smiling when saying no is much more powerful than saying it with a sour—or even scary—face. But to get there, I had to first make a conscious effort to put off harshness and put on gentleness.

So now it's your turn. Go out and add gentleness to who you are today. You'll be surprised at how it improves your relationships.

Father, make me aware of when I'm being harsh and abrasive with others. Help me replace that habit with a spirit of gentleness that makes other people feel safe and accepted around me.

April 23

Put On Patience

Growing in Christ often comes down to things we take off and things we put on. It's like when we say to a child, "Hold on—just be patient!" What we're really telling them is "Put on some patience." Well, what exactly does that mean?

The Bible often talks about patience as being willing to delay something you want on behalf of someone else's need. And that's just the way God is with us: merciful, patient, slow to judge, and long-suffering.

You put on patience when you let a child finish a task in their own way, not yours. You're being long-suffering when you refuse to give up on a family member who has given up on you. You show mercy and restraint when you keep on loving someone in your home who isn't acting very lovable. And every time you practice putting on patience, you grow a little bit more like Christ.

Where would I be without the patience you've shown me, Lord? I ask you to help me learn the discipline of treating my family members with the kind of patience that puts their interests ahead of my own.

Put On Self-Control

"Get ahold of yourself!"

Ever felt like saying that to a friend or relative? A lot of people in our world today act like they're a helpless victim of their circumstances and experiences. They fall prey to their passions, their desires, and their emotions. But getting ahold of yourself—or learning self-control—is about taking command of your tongue, your selfish desires, your fears . . . and not letting them run rampant on you.

A parent who doesn't follow through with discipline because they feel guilty about something in their life. An employee who cuts corners because "everyone else does it." A teenager who talks back to a stepparent because they're really frustrated with their mom or dad. All of these people are failing to exercise self-control.

Instead of playing the role of a victim, ask God to help you get ahold of yourself, to put on some self-control. After he does that, you just might like yourself better. And other people will, for sure.

Father, help me practice self-control every day rather than allowing my circumstances, emotions, or other people's behavior to control me.

Par for the Stepfamily Course

I n golf terms, when you shoot par for the course, that means you're doing pretty good. When stepfamilies ask, "Is this normal?" what they're really asking is, "Are we doing okay?" Jennifer wrote to me worried about the different levels of openness her kids felt toward their stepfather of four years. She wondered if it was normal for kids to feel so differently from each other.

You see, part of her problem was comparing her blended family to a first family, where it's normal for kids to feel generally the same about their parent. But when it comes to a stepfamily, I'd have to say, "Yes, Jennifer. This is normal. And they don't have to feel the same; just let each relationship stand on its own."

I might also add, "Yep, this is par for the stepfamily course. Which means you're doing okay."

Give me the wisdom to recognize that our blended family will have some aspects that are unique to stepfamilies. Help me avoid the comparison trap and patiently wait for each relationship to grow and develop on its own timetable.

April 26

Divine Help for Negative Attacks

W hat do we do? My husband's ex is so negative about us that it's really hurting our relationship with his kids."

One of the most menacing attacks on any single-parent or stepfamily home is a difficult ex-spouse or extended family member who makes it feel like you have a terrorist living next door.

The temptation is to get drawn into their devious game and try to outfox the fox. That's only human nature. But of course, that never works. What could work is praying that God would soften their heart and help them understand that they are only hurting their children. And to pray that they would find a way to release whatever bitterness is fueling their critical behavior.

Pray for yourself, too. Ask God to help you endure the persecution and to give wisdom as you decide how to respond, day in and day out, to the negativity thrown at you. A good place to start is by meditating on Romans 12:21: "Do not be overcome by evil, but overcome evil with good."

Lord, I ask for wisdom and strength to respond in a godly way to criticism and unfair attacks.

Make the First Move

When people have their backs turned toward each other, who makes the first move? I know a stepmom who has good relationships with most of her stepchildren, but she and her stepdaughter are just plain stuck. They can't seem to move forward. You see, there's been a lot of water under the bridge—muddied, turbulent water.

When this stepmom shared their story, she admitted how they had each hurt the other. Then she and I decided that first, she needed to cut her stepdaughter a break. The stepdaughter's disrespectful behavior isn't really personal; she's just trying to make sense of the changes in her life.

Second, the stepmom needs to keep setting firm boundaries, but do so with a smile.

And third, she needs to forgive her stepdaughter for a few things so she can make the first move toward reconciliation. Why her? Because when your back is turned toward another person, the first one responsible to turn back around is always you.

Examine my heart, God, and reveal to me anyone I've turned my back on. Then show me how to make the first move toward reconciliation and restoration.

Bless Your Kids' Stepparent

Aren't moms and stepmoms supposed to despise each other? In our culture I guess we're not too surprised when a biological mother and stepmother clash with each other. It just seems natural for there to be a sour competition between them. And we've all seen television shows and movies portraying these women as enemies.

So imagine how surprised Tiana felt one day when her stepson's mom told her how glad she was for Tiana to be in his life. Say what? Tiana called it a miracle and considered the conversation a tremendous blessing. In the end, it inspired her to be more cooperative with the mom and even more attentive to her stepson than she had been before.

Did you catch that? That's what can happen when we die to ourselves and make an effort to bless others. Peace reigns, kids benefit, and God is glorified. It's a win-win-win situation.

Lord, help me bless my children by being a blessing to members of their other family, speaking words of affirmation, appreciation, and encouragement.

Embrace Opportunities for Healing

S ometimes announcing an engagement can be an opportunity to find forgiveness. That might sound strange, but have you ever noticed how transitions in life naturally create opportunities for healing? For example, becoming a parent helps you forgive your parents because you now understand how hard parenting is. Coming to the end of life is a huge motivator for many to bury the hatchet and reconcile a broken relationship.

Divorced parents may not fully understand how hurt their children were by the divorce until they announce a new marriage. For kids, a parent's engagement awakens old wounds and squashes their hope that their parents will reconcile. Other family transitions can do this as well: having a baby, a death in the family, a child's graduation, a deployment, or moving to a new city.

Instead of getting defensive about the past, recognize that the transition has created an opportunity. A chance to listen to the other person's hurt, to ask for forgiveness, and to heal your relationship.

Father, help me stay watchful for any opportunities to strengthen or heal damaged and broken relationships.

Learn the Language of Heaven

Love is the language of heaven. In 1 Corinthians 13 Paul tells us that love is what lasts from this life into the next one. When Christ comes again, love will be made perfect. That means that love is our destiny because it is the very essence of God, revealed to us through the person of Jesus Christ.

Noted Bible scholar N.T. Wright says that love is the language spoken in God's world, the music played in God's courts. And we are invited right now—in this life—to learn it and to practice it.[12] Now, on a practical level, your marriage and family relationships are the practice field on which you learn the qualities, habits, and disciplines of love that you will take with you to heaven.

So spend some time today learning the language of heaven as you interact with your spouse and children.

Father God, show me the best ways to immerse myself in learning the language of love until I speak it fluently to my family members.

Whom Do You Trust?

When things get really tough, your default mode should be to run straight into the arms of God. According to family therapist Terry Hargrave, marriage and family relationships have three sources of truth: God, mature trusted friends or mentors, and yourself. But trust yourself only after years of walking with God and learning about his will and his Word. Until then, selfishness is likely to get in the way.

But whom do you trust if your relationship is in distress? Let me suggest you default back to trusting mostly in God, and some in mentors or counselors. Not in yourself. Pain and fear can distort our viewpoints. We tend to see ourselves as a victim, with others at fault. Doubt colors how we judge them and the glass seems half-empty. And that's never helpful.

So even though it's hard, set aside your judgment and default to God's wisdom. Repent of any wrongdoing, ask for and grant forgiveness, and extend a hand of grace. That's how you get back on track.

Father, I trust your wisdom above all other sources. Help me use your Word as the basis to evaluate advice from others as well as my own opinions.

Rest in His Love

Ever thought about how being loved by God helps you love others? The two greatest commands laid out by Jesus in Matthew 22:36–40 are entwined: loving God and being loved by God helps us to love others, and vice versa.

For example, when I rest in my love relationship with God, I won't idolize or be dependent on a partner's love for me, because I'm already deeply loved by my Creator. Conflict will sting a little less. Apologies will come more quickly. Forgiveness will be easier to extend. And self-respect will show itself in both sacrifice and sometimes saying no.

In stepfamilies, resting in God's love provides stability even when there's a lot of confusion and uncertainty. It gives you a sense of worth even when initially rejected by new family members. So in difficult family relationships, don't try to force the feelings you know you should have. Instead, let your love for others flow out of God's love for you.

Teach me how to love others not on the basis of my feelings, but as a response to the great love and mercy that you have lavished on me.

Stay Off the Teeter-Totter

Parents need to get off the teeter-totter. Let me explain. Have you ever been in a conversation where the other person's position prompts you to take a more extreme polar-opposite position from theirs? You know, to counterbalance their point of view? Normally you wouldn't take that position, but because they went down, you went up.

This becomes a snare for some parents: One parent is a little strict so the other becomes a little permissive . . . so the other becomes even more strict, leading the other to be even more permissive. When one goes down, the other goes up. In the end, both are stuck in extreme postures they wouldn't normally take and the relationship is out of balance.

If a parent and stepparent don't get off the teeter-totter, their parenting will suffer—and so will their marriage. So stop trying to counterbalance the other. Move toward the middle, and together you will find balance to keep you steady.

Keep us from the tendency to automatically take opposing positions from each other. Instead, help us think about issues and problems calmly and rationally, finding the perfect balance in our parenting and our marital relationship.

Boomerang Children

Know what happens when a boomerang child leaves your home? That's right—they come back. It's happening more and more in our culture. Young adult children leave home with the best of intentions, only to end up returning. Now, if this has happened to you, you know the boundaries around this are confusing for everyone. Parents find themselves walking the line between life coach and landlord. And children who are trying to be on their own find themselves a lot more dependent than they'd like to be.

Stepparents in this situation—who may not have lived with the young adult very much—can find themselves totally lost. So start addressing this as a couple by clarifying your expectations. Once you agree, share them with the boomerang child and then listen to their needs. Your goal is to trust God as you honor your marriage covenant, while at the same time helping the child plant their feet back on the path to independence.

As our children grow, Lord, show us how to train them to become responsible, independent adults. If they end up returning home, help us set healthy boundaries that will encourage them as they make a fresh start.

Redeeming Our Story

Notice that title? That's pretty much what God does. He redeems us from ourselves.

As a matter of fact, the entire Bible shares one redemptive story after another. Through Noah God redeemed the world from utter evil. In Joseph God redeemed what his brothers meant for evil. In the second Adam, Christ, God redeemed what the first Adam had taken away by allowing sin to enter the world.

Thankfully, God is still redeeming people's stories today. Recently I talked with a prominent Christian recording artist who readily acknowledged the negative impact his parents' divorce had had on him. It left a troubling residue all over his life. But years later, God began to weave together threads of healing and restoration. Now this recording artist has a new story to tell the world.

No, you can't change your past. But God can change the story you get to tell about your past. Regardless of your background, you can trust him to redeem your story.

Thank you, God, for being in the business of redeeming people from the shame and pain of their pasts. Bring healing into our family so our stories can reflect your mercy and grace.

Celebrating Stepparents

Here's a headline you haven't read in the media lately: "Good News . . . about Stepparents!" If you're like me, you probably have a few Google alerts set up so you can stay in touch with subjects you care about. I have some alerts set up for the keywords *stepmom* and *stepdad*. And I have to tell you, rarely—if ever—do I see online media coverage about either term that is positive or encouraging.

Come on! Really? Not only is that not accurate, it supports the myth that stepparents are evil and to be feared. One boy told me, "He's only been my father for about six years. But even when he disciplines me, I can tell he still loves me. That's why I'm nominating him for the Father of the Year award."

All over the world there are stepparents who day in and day out are giving, nurturing, teaching, and loving—and if you ask me, worthy of an award. Why can't we tweet *that*? We need to set the record straight.

Father, help us not to hold back, but to celebrate one another and the good things that happen in our home.

Love with Maturity

I recently observed a mature love moment in action—and I learned a lot. Here's what happened: A friend of mine witnessed a social injustice and courageously stood up against it. When his wife heard about what he'd done, they happened to be standing near a small group of people. In front of everyone, she instantly reacted and jumped down his throat for putting himself in what could have been a dangerous situation.

Naturally, the poor guy could have gotten defensive or embarrassed that others were looking on as his wife chastised him. But instead he responded gently, acknowledging that she had reacted that way out of concern for his safety.

Here's the lesson: Mature friends and lovers stay emotionally connected to people who are mad at them; they don't run away or hide, but calmly stay attuned to the angry person. Because they focus on the other person, they can tell when anger is actually concern in disguise. They recognize a loving spirit even when they're being personally attacked. Now that's loving others like Jesus did.

Father, instead of instinctively reacting to anger from a loved one, help me recognize and respond to that person's motivation and needs.

The Danger of Overprotecting

Kids in stepfamilies go through a lot. Which is one reason it's so easy for a parent to become overprotective. One stepdad dealing with this issue came to me and poured out his heart: "My wife is so protective of her kids. She blocks me from asking them to do things and she goes behind my back."

Hey parents, I get it. When your child has been through a lot, you naturally want to protect them. But when you constantly hover over your kids to guide and guard them, when you continually tell the stepparent how to act, or when you defend your kids at all costs—well, then you're just causing a new set of problems. A new set of problems that, ironically, will hurt your kids. You see, when you treat them as fragile, you keep them fragile.

If you want to really help your kids, be their parent, not their overprotector.

Lord, show me how to parent my kids in ways that build up their self-esteem and encourage them to grow into stable, responsible adults.

Laugh!

Wise stepparents know that laughter is good medicine for their family. When asked what her advice to stepfamilies would be, one stepmom said, "Laugh and be silly because there are rough times. There are struggles and obstacles and tears, but if you can laugh as a family you'll find your way through."

Research has shown that laughing brings many physical and emotional benefits. It reduces tension in stressful situations, and it lightens the mood when relationships are anxious. But more important, a sense of humor helps you not to take yourself—or your circumstances—so seriously. As this stepmom pointed out, finding a way to chuckle even in the midst of struggle will help you survive the moment. It will give you the strength to press on.

So look for opportunities to encourage your family to laugh together. After all, Proverbs 17:22 tells us that a joyful or cheerful heart is good medicine. Sometimes laughter is just what the Great Physician ordered.

Help us find healthy ways to build laughter into our conversations and family activities.

A Face Hard to Love

Ever heard the phrase, "Now that's a face only a parent could love"? Well, what if you're a stepparent seeing a face that you can't love very easily? Of course, I'm not talking about their actual physical face. I'm thinking about a stepchild with a huge attitude problem, or one who continually lies. Or maybe that "child" is a lazy twenty-eight-year-old who eats up all your food.

I'm simply being honest here. Some kids are just plain harder to love than others. So, what to do if you find yourself faced with this challenge? First and foremost, pray. Don't just pray *about* them—pray *for* them. And ask God to give you the strength and grace to love them.

Second step: Keep searching until you find one interest that the two of you share in common and then build on it. It may not seem like much in the beginning, but at least it's a start. And pretty soon, you might find yourself wondering why you ever thought that face was hard to love.

Father, thank you for loving me even when I'm not so lovable. Help me cherish each member of our family, regardless of the challenges involved.

Reducing Cholesterol in Your Marriage

We all know that high cholesterol is bad for your body. It builds up in your arteries and blocks blood flow. In your marriage, cholesterol is the harmful stuff that builds up and blocks communication and emotional intimacy. Here's a tip for reducing it: Double-check your attitude. Research shows that unhappy couples in blended families are often more jealous, critical, controlling, and stubborn. By contrast, happy couples are far less likely to demonstrate these negative qualities.[13] Instead, each one lives and loves on behalf of the other—or maybe I should say, on behalf of their "us-ness."

Healthy marriages are made in part by two people who regularly double-check the "cholesterol" in their marriage. And they're mindful that what they say and how they act each day either contributes to a healthy "us-ness" or takes away from it.

Do you want a healthy blended marriage? Then love large with your whole heart, cholesterol-free.

God, help me regularly examine my attitudes, speech, and behavior toward my spouse, replacing destructive habits with ones that contribute to the health and intimacy of our relationship.

Feed Your Wife

Here's a question for husbands: Just how fat is your wife? Okay, maybe I should clarify what I mean by that. I'm really asking, How fat *with your love* is your wife? In Ephesians 5:25–33, God urges us men through the apostle Paul to nourish and cherish our wives. Some translations tell us to feed and care for our wives like we feed and care for our own bodies.

I've often thought that if I loved my wife the way I feed my body, she should be at least pleasantly plump with love. Believe me, this is the one and only case where she'd really like to be "fat." So, the next time you stick some food in your mouth, ask yourself, "How well am I feeding and caring for my wife these days?" Do your best to nourish her the way Ephesians 5 instructs, and believe me, she'll eat it up.

Father, teach me to be the kind of husband whose wife lives each day knowing beyond a shadow of a doubt that she is deeply loved.

Stepparents Need a Hug

One stepmom was pleasantly surprised when her two oldest step-daughters gave her a card on Mother's Day that read, "Everyone needs a back-up mom. You're mine!" What a huge compliment—she was beaming from ear to ear. She knows how hard it is for kids and adult children alike to honor their stepmom without dishonoring their biological mother, or feeling disloyal to her. So, why the need for the hug?

Because this stepmom's other two stepchildren didn't acknowledge her at all on Mother's Day. Not a word.

So what's your situation? Are you accepted or rejected? A part of the family or pushed aside? Maybe you're both. Talk about confusing. I guess you could say that ambiguity is a stepparent's middle name. And that's why they need a hug.

(A prayer for the biological parent to pray over the stepparent. If you're both stepparents take turns praying over each other.) Father, thank you for my partner who has taken on the task of loving and caring for my children. I am grateful for all they do. Please strengthen them for the challenges they face and give us wisdom as a couple to parent well together. Amen.

Your Story's Not Over Yet

You've been more of a mom to me than my real mom, so . . . can I call you Mom?"

If you want to talk about music to a stepmom's ears, that would be her favorite lyric: "Can I call you Mom?" Now here's the backstory. The journey began when the stepdaughter was just thirteen. The early years were difficult and hurtful, but this stepmom pressed through, determined to find her way.

She attended my stepfamily conference and read books. She and her husband helped with a small group for stepcouples in their church. To put it simply, she just kept on living and loving. And now, fifteen years later, her twenty-eight-year-old stepdaughter asks, "Can I call you Mom?"

Are you still in the "difficult and hurtful" stage today? Then take heart from this stepmom's story. Be patient and hang on. Keep going. Love isn't done with your story yet.

Lord Jesus, help me keep pressing forward and being the best parent I can be, trusting that my efforts are helping write a happy ending for our family story.

Note to Self

Mom always said there'd be days like this. "Days like what?" you might ask. Days when you're discouraged.

You know, we do this funny thing to ourselves. Before having kids we dream about who they will become; once they arrive we worry about who they *might* become. Before marriage we notice the best about the other person; afterward we tend to focus on the bad. And so we get discouraged about all the negatives in our present circumstances and all the potential negatives the future might bring.

What can really help us out on these days is a change in our perspective. Some people keep a list of positive things—notes to self, if you will—that can transform their attitude during times of discouragement and disappointment. An encouraging note from a friend. A positive story about your spouse. Or reminders of the good times with your stepchildren. Anything you can go to when things are stressful to help you remember that it's not all bad, and that God is still working.

Father, help each one of us store up memories of good times and positive affirmations to help change our perspective on days when we feel discouraged.

Come Together

It's Not by Councience this is happening its by GODS DIVINE PURPOSE

As parents, when you find yourselves on different sides of an issue, it's crucial that you come together. To be a strong team, it's important for parents to be unified. But it's *extremely* important for a parent and stepparent to come together. One way you can do that is to hold your criticism and listen to the other's perspective.

Adam was looking forward to his kids coming for the weekend, but his wife—their stepmother, Monica—was concerned about all the tension she would face. Instead of criticizing her for being pessimistic, as he normally did, Adam learned to listen and connect to her need. "I can tell you're anxious about the weekend. What can we do to make things go a little more smoothly for you?"

With this approach, Adam and Monica have a chance to come together. And once they make that choice, not just the weekend, but the marriage will likely go more smoothly.

> *Lord, help me learn to see things from my mate's perspective so that we can come together to meet each other's needs and be unified in our marriage and our parenting.*

Just REMEMBER GOD Say's.....

I MAKE All Thing's Work 2together for the GooD. HE Does Not say I work thing's for the Bad. OR to harm You. So Know

Be a Firefighter

Every couple on earth faces conflict. In fact, both healthy and unhealthy couples experience about the same amount. The difference between them is how they manage it. Our research shows that healthy couples are almost six times more likely to resolve their arguments than unhealthy couples are.[14] That leads to the natural question: How do they manage that?

Essentially, they practice dozens of disciplines that help move the discussion toward resolution. One of those essential techniques is managing their tongues. James 3:5 warns that our words can be like a spark that sets off a forest fire. Not criticizing your spouse, managing your tone, turning down your volume, and listening with openness to understand your spouse are the kinds of disciplines that keep you from setting off a destructive, raging fire in your relationship.

So don't be a fire starter. Instead, be a firefighter who puts them out.

Teach me to control my tongue so that I speak words that encourage and build up rather than words that spark arguments and conflict.

I love you & Maybe Watch the Movie Couragous or Fireproof

Time for a Sonic Run!

You know what I love? I love it when our family is in the car and my wife declares, "Hey, it's happy hour. It's time for a Sonic run!" Rituals are simple behaviors that we repeat on a fairly regular basis. Making a "Sonic run" is one of ours. Now, as good as that cherry limeade tastes, there's something else going on that's far more important than enjoying a refreshing drink.

When families share a ritual, it creates a connection point. And over time, those repeated connections build memories, create a sense of togetherness, and bond you together as family members. Can you see why this is so important to blended families? Be intentional to create and maintain rituals that connect. Share a favorite food, tell a joke every day before school, or play a family game after dinner.

And next time you're in the car, why not make a Sonic run (or something similar) of your own?

> *Give us ideas for adding rituals and habits that will create meaningful memories for our family and help us enjoy each other's company.*

Part-Time Parenting

When you're a part-time parent to your biological kids, it's amazing what matters—and what doesn't. Take Eric, for example. He's a stickler about drink coasters. He insists that everyone in the family use one—*except, that is, for his biological kids*. You see, Eric only gets to see his kids a few days a month. He's anxious for his children to *want* to come back, so somehow he doesn't notice if they use a drink coaster or not.

But his wife notices that he doesn't notice. And she resents it. My advice to Eric would be: Guests to your home should get a free pass from using a coaster, but your children aren't guests. Yes, they're part-time. And yes, you want them to enjoy being there. But they're probably not as fragile as you fear. Plus, you can't have a double standard for your stepkids and your kids and expect peace and harmony to reign in your household.

Now pass your kids a coaster and say, "Welcome home."

Lord, open my eyes to any hint of a double standard in how I treat my biological children and stepchildren. Help us create an environment where everyone feels at home and accepted.

Healing Your Bruises

Have you ever gotten the feeling that your relationships are doing a number on you?

Well, maybe that's because they are! God, in his infinite wisdom, has orchestrated the challenges of marriage and personal relationships to grow us up. Those difficulties and trials help us learn to love like Jesus. Now here's the cool thing: The growing-up process also helps us overcome our bruises. You know, the hurts and heartaches that we all experience in life.

You see, one antidote to a disappointing relationship is a healthy relationship. It recalibrates your experience of love from a place of hurt to one of safety and comfort.

But there's the catch: You have to be in a growing, intimate relationship in order to experience healing. That takes courage after being hurt, but it's truly worth the risk.

So, do you want to heal some bruises? Dance like no one's watching and love like you've got nothing to lose.

Lord Jesus, help me see the trials and difficulties in relationships as opportunities to mature and become more like you. Give me the courage to open myself up to all that you have to teach me.

Help Children Grieve

One family topic not discussed enough is how to help children grieve well. And that's too bad because unfortunately, sometimes children are just plain forgotten. When my twelve-year-old son died, my wife and I struggled to help our other two sons grieve the loss of their brother. We soon learned that siblings are often the forgotten mourners when a child dies. Parents get lots of attention, but frequently, siblings are overlooked.

I've found that to be true, to varying degrees, in many other situations as well. When a parent dies, we speak to the widow, not the child. When a parent is ready to remarry, the child's grief is secondary to the couple's happy news. And when co-parents battle over money or visitation schedules, how it affects their child is often completely forgotten.

For your child's sake, don't pretend like the loss isn't there anymore. It is. Acknowledge it and speak to the child about it. Let them know *you* haven't forgotten.

Father, make me sensitive to the needs of children who are grieving a death or struggling with another type of loss or major life transition.

Create a Financial Plan for Your Step-Money

When it comes to stepfamilies, there's not a one-size-fits-all estate plan. The unique dynamics of blended families create some very unique financial situations as well. For example, did you know that long after a divorce, an ex-spouse will almost always be entitled to a portion of your retirement or stock options?

And imagine this scenario: You get married and have kids, then pass away. If your widow remarries and then she passes away, did you know that some of your assets could end up going to her surviving spouse and not to your children? That's probably not part of your plan for your resources, right?

Here's the point: Don't leave your financial matters unattended. You need to come together with your spouse and settle on a plan. Pray together, meet with an attorney, and put it down on paper. Every estate plan will be different. You just need to get yours mapped out.

Lord God, guide us and give us wisdom to know how to create a financial plan that will be the best fit for our family.

Summer Sleepover: Sending and Receiving

Do your kids have an extended summer visitation schedule? If so, would you like to know how to start it off right? Helping your kids with the "summer sleepover" depends on whether you're sending or receiving. If you're sending: Schedule a pre-summer conference call with the other household to learn how to help your child pack for summer activities. Then when the time comes, send them off with your permission to fully enjoy their stay.

If you're on the receiving end: Plan some special activities around their arrival. You might even carve out some extra time for them to be with the biological parent. Then settle into your typical summer routine while trying to make the most of this precious time you share.

And finally, whether you're sending or receiving, what kids need most from you is a good attitude about making the summer schedule work. Doing your part—with joy and peace in your heart—can really bless your kids.[15]

Help us make plans for the summer months that create joy-filled memories and strengthen family relationships.

Graduation of a Family

Here's a pop quiz: What do a graduation, a new job, a career promotion, getting married, getting pregnant, having a baby, or having a grandbaby all have in common? They're all moments that tell us we've graduated to a new season of life. Each of these events announces that a major transition has occurred; we understand that from now on, life as we know it will be different.

I've often wondered how stepfamilies know when they've graduated to become a family. I mean, in the beginning you're a collection of people from different families who are figuring out how to be a family. But at some point, you figure it out and a stepparent starts acting like a parent and stepsiblings start pestering each other just like biological brothers and sisters do.

Well, so far society offers no formal graduation ceremony for becoming a family. But maybe you can just act like there is—and you just got your diploma.

Heavenly Father, even though each one of us is a work in progress, we know that we have received our diploma as a family. Help us find joy in this season of life as we continue our education at your hands.

May 25

Parental Blind Spots

Have you ever seen a parent turn a blind eye to their child's poor behavior and wondered, *How can they not see what their child is doing?* I know I have. Then I realized that one reason we close our eyes to our kids' behavior is that we're used to it. I can grow so accustomed to my kids' behavior that I don't notice it anymore. But other people sure do.

In blended families, sometimes the stepparent notices a child's misbehavior more quickly than the biological parent does. And if they say something about it, the biological parent might even defend their kid, saying, "It's no big deal." This is a real trap for stepcouples because it pits you against one another.

We all have strengths and weaknesses as parents. And because of that, all parents need friends who will speak the truth about their blind spots. Parents and stepparents can also do that for each other. Remember: God intended parenting to be at least a two-person team. So lay down your defensiveness and listen to each other.

Lord, help us parent as a team with the honesty and trust needed to help each other identify our blind spots.

Shift the Outsider In

"I'm such an outsider. How do I get in?"

Whether it means feeling like a social outcast in junior high or not fitting in at church, nobody likes to be an outsider. Yet all stepparents begin their blended family journey as outsiders. Their spouse is already an insider with their kids, while the stepparent has to find a way to gain acceptance.

Here's an idea: Find activities that help move the stepparent in.[16] Let's say you're planning to spend Saturday afternoon playing softball, but the stepparent isn't athletic at all. They're just going to look foolish and even worse, continue to feel like they don't—or can't—belong.

So instead, choose an activity they can do well with the kids. Something that gives them a chance to connect and build memories. Even if it's something the biological parent doesn't do well, you're still better off. Because anytime you make an effort to draw the outsider in, your circle grows stronger.

Lead us to activities that will draw in those family members who feel like outsiders. Help our circle of loved ones grow ever stronger as we keep you at the center.

Break Free from Guilt

Yes, Ron, this marriage and family are much better than my first— and I feel guilty about it."

That may sound a little odd, but that's what some divorced and remarried people feel, even though they probably don't admit it. And as part of their church family, we certainly don't help when we reveal a condescending attitude. The message often comes through loud and clear: "You had a failed marriage so *you're* a failure—and you don't deserve to be happy now."

Wait a minute. I thought there was no condemnation for those who are in Christ Jesus (Romans 8:1). Aren't all of us relying on that truth? Yes, sin is dark and has consequences in this life. But that doesn't mean a repentant heart can't rest in the warmth of God's mercy and grace.

So go ahead and rest in it. And help others rest in it, too. Free of condemnation and free of shame. And free of secret guilt.

Merciful Father, remove any trace of guilt and feelings of failure over the past. Teach me how to rest in your lavish mercy and grace, which free me to fully live in the present.

Weep and Rejoice

Romans 12:15 tells us to "rejoice with those who rejoice, weep with those who weep." Sometimes we have to do them both at the same time.

Everyone who has experienced a loss knows that special celebrations and occasions like Mother's Day and Father's Day can bring out mixed emotions. It works that way in stepfamilies, too. Family members once fractured by divorce might rejoice over new family members who have entered their lives, while at the same time others weep over being separated from someone they love.

It can all get pretty confusing. But I think the secret is learning to go with the flow. Being mindfully present in the moment and making space for loved ones to be happy one minute and sad the next—all while not taking their sadness personally—is a wonderful gift you can offer to those around you. In fact, rejoicing and weeping together might just be the best gift you could give, or receive.

Lord, during special days keep me sensitive to family members who are struggling with heavy or conflicted emotions. Show me the best ways to offer comfort and understanding.

Keep Looking Ahead

When the marital going gets tough, the tough get going—in their marriage. The weak? They look back and decide they made a mistake.

Let's be honest, we've all been discouraged with our marriages. But discouragement is not the issue; it's what you do with it that matters. For example, when the dedicated person experiences discouragement, it simply motivates them to keep working on their marriage.

Then there are others who stay focused on the past, constantly gazing backward and wondering if they made a mistake. They might question their decision-making process or dissect the dating process, but ultimately this just adds to the discouragement.

So admit that back then, you didn't know what you didn't know. And truthfully, what you didn't know doesn't matter anymore, because now you've made a commitment. And commitment expresses itself in the here and now; it's not dictated by the past.

If your marriage is struggling, ask for God's help and seek out someone to provide direction and support. Don't look back. Keep looking forward.

Father, whenever I feel discouraged about my marriage, help me look to the future with a renewed commitment and determination.

Summer Sleepover: Stepparent Advice

It's time for the annual extended "summer sleepover"—but if you're a stepparent getting ready to host stepchildren who primarily live in another home, you may feel in some ways like you're starting over from scratch. It's true, stepparent-stepchild relationships do take "one step backward" when you've had extended time apart during the school year. So the extended summer visitation can be a little intimidating.

First, take a deep breath. And start with what you have. Reconnect with your stepchildren through common interests and maybe a few special fun activities. But be sure to pay attention to their pace. If they pursue time with you, then freely give it. If they seem distant and need time to warm up, honor that. Find simple ways of connecting, but never force yourself on them. Hopefully, they'll soon warm up like the weather, and then the summer fun can really begin![17]

> *Give me patience to allow my stepchildren to adjust to their summer home on their own schedule, and ideas to help them feel as secure and comfortable as possible.*

Wear Your Labels Proudly

"Ron, what do we do? My kids are confusing my husband."

We all have different roles in life, don't we? And each of our roles has a separate label. I'm a dad, husband, son, brother—you understand. Suzanne wrote to us because her kids were confusing her husband with the labels they use. The youngest child calls him Dad, but the middle son refuses to address him that way. He prefers to use his first name. And the oldest daughter refers to him as "my stepdad." So Mom's confused. The stepdad's confused.

Well, since terms tend to reflect emotional bonds and loyalty conflicts in children, this mom and stepdad should learn to be okay with all three labels. As long as the terms are respectful, they can just accept the situation and work with it.

As always, the best approach is to just focus on being Christlike. And remember that the labels will change over time, but the relationship will endure.

Lord Jesus, keep us from obsessing over what name labels are used in our family. Instead, help us be more focused on our identity in you.

Love Makes Room for All

"Ron, I'm jealous of a ten-year-old and I resent her like crazy."

This stepdad felt like his wife's relationship with her daughter was getting in the way of his relationship with his wife. Not an unusual sentiment. In stepfamilies, it's fairly common for people to feel jealous of someone or something that seems to have taken their place. What they actually feel deep down is fear and insecurity. If their jealousy could talk, it would say, "I want to feel important and I'm afraid you took my place."

But here's the rub: If you act on the basis of those jealous feelings, over time you'll likely become bitter, critical, and competitive. And then you will lose your place for sure. On the other hand, if you ask God to give you compassion for the person and then act on that, you just might discover that love leaves more than enough room for everyone involved to be important.

Father, help us create a family atmosphere of acceptance, love, and compassion that drives away feelings of insecurity and jealousy and makes each family member feel valued and cherished.

Capture Those Moments

So who's in your family portrait? We all use pictures and videos to capture the moments of our lives. And family portraits tell a story about who is in our family at different seasons of our lives. For example, stepparents sometimes feel left out when looking at pictures of their spouse with their previous family. And kids may feel alienated when their visitation schedule didn't allow them to be part of a fun video moment.

You want to make sure to document your new family story so people can begin to include one another in that story. Be intentional to take pictures and videos of your blended family. Then organize them and make them available through social media channels, or maybe in a good old-fashioned photo album.

When there are new faces in the frame, make sure to capture the moments they share, and then share those moments.

Help us effectively use pictures and videos as tools not only to document our family story but also to strengthen family relationships and smooth the way during times of transition.

Jump Out of That Rut

Remember those old vinyl record albums? Here's a bit of trivia: How many grooves are there on a twelve-inch record? The answer: only one. Sounds surprising, but there's only one long, continuous rut. That's why the needle moves inward as the record plays.

You know, when it comes to the ruts of our life, we can get stuck in one long continuous pattern. We choose the same bad friends, make the same poor decisions, and find ourselves stuck in the same type of relationships. Pretty soon the rut is continually leading us where we don't want to end up. The question becomes: How do we skip out of that rut?

James says the transformation comes when we obey God's Word. "But be doers of the word, and not hearers only, deceiving yourselves" (James 1:22). Not taking action means staying stuck in an old rut. But obedience to righteousness brings about growth and change.

I ask your Holy Spirit to work within me, helping me break free from harmful ruts as I obey your Word and pattern my life after your guidelines for living in righteousness.

Daddy-Daughter Dance

I know a man who didn't get to walk his daughter down the aisle, but he did get to take part in the Daddy-Daughter dance. After nearly twenty years of being a stepdad, my friend saw how his stepdaughter was struggling to decide who should walk her down the aisle on her wedding day. Should it be her dad, who had been in and out of her life, or her stepdad, who had been a faithful presence all along?

Once again my friend blessed his stepdaughter by putting her needs and welfare ahead of his own feelings. He let her know he would be okay with her father walking her down the aisle, if that should be her decision. His words brought a light to her eyes and a smile to her face. And then she insisted, "But nobody's going to take away our dance at the reception."

You'd better believe that stepdad enjoyed their Daddy-Daughter dance. He loved every single minute of it!

Lord, help me focus not on the things I've missed out on in my child's life, but on all that we have shared and will share in the future.

The Fun Factor, Part 1

You don't have to be a brain surgeon to guess that having fun together as a couple is good for your marriage. My friends Ty and Andrea met on a tennis court. They secretly watched each other play in a club league for months before Ty finally asked Andrea to play a match—and they turned out to be a match themselves. Fast-forward a few years and the fun activities that originally brought them together have now faded away amid life's busyness.

Making time for leisure activities is important for all marriages, but research has discovered that it's especially important for stepfamily couples.[18] There's just something about the fun factor, as I call it, that helps protect you from the stress of stepfamily life and strengthen your relationship.

So go ahead—maybe it's time to hit that tennis court once again. Love-Love!

Help us remember the activities and fun we shared in the beginning of our relationship, and show us how to make new memories that we can cherish in the future.

The Fun Factor, Part 2

G uess what? A regular diet of fun predicts whether stepfamily couples will have a dynamic, fulfilling relationship or an unhappy, dissatisfied one. (I'm sure I can guess which one you prefer.) Of course this makes sense, right? Couples who engage in leisure activities together on a regular basis report that they like each other and enjoy being with one another. That seems like such a no-brainer. So why don't we find time for the fun factor more often?

Part of the problem is that one-third of stepfamily couples disagree about what constitutes a good time. They have different personal interests and hobbies that pull them in different directions. Now, it's okay for a husband and wife to have different interests, but you must also find something you can share together.

Hobbies and leisure time keep Jack from being a dull boy. Sharing them with Jill keeps their marriage from being dull, too.

Guide us as we learn to carve out time in our schedules for special activities that we can enjoy together as a couple.

The Fun Factor, Part 3

The past couple of days we've talked about maximizing the fun factor in your marriage. But sometimes the path to fun is full of sacrifice. Let me tell you about Ed and Virginia. Ed enjoys golf, while Virginia loves to window shop and hunt for antiques. And neither one of them enjoys what the other enjoys. (Ah, Houston, we have a problem.)

It's not a bad thing that they each have their own leisure time. But what separates poor or mediocre marriages from great ones—especially in stepfamilies—is engaging each other in shared fun. And to get there, Ed and Virginia are going to have to sacrifice what they prefer in order to connect with each other around something they both enjoy.

Now here's the beauty of God's intended design for marriage: When each one makes sacrifices for the other, there's a balance in their relationship. And part of the end result is shared fun.

Lord, make me willing to give up my personal preferences when I need to focus on my spouse's wishes and desires. Help us keep a balance in our marriage so we can reflect your design.

Learn Some New Steps

We all struggle with figuring out how to deal with difficult people. Well, I've got one tip that just might be the biggest secret weapon of all. If you find yourself in an ongoing conflict with a difficult person, start by noticing your part of the dance. And then change your steps.

Before I elaborate, I have to tell you that this takes a great deal of humility and emotional maturity. It's really easy to focus on how the other person is acting and to diagnose their problems, but *you* always play a role in a sticky situation. For example, any time you try to change a stubborn neighbor, friend, spouse, or an ex-spouse, you automatically invite resistance from them. By pushing your own agenda, you set the stage for them to be the very thing that drives you crazy. Doesn't make much sense, does it?

Caught in a difficult relationship? Start by changing *you*.

Whenever I clash with someone, Lord, open my eyes to see how I contribute to the problem and how I can learn ways to resolve the conflict.

Make the Hard Choices

Sometimes we parents have to give up what we really, really want in order to give our children what they really, really need. I once heard about a blended family couple who applied for a job with a nonprofit ministry. They were highly qualified and eager to serve the Lord with their talents. But there was one complication: Taking the job would mean moving to another city far away from the husband's son, who lived with his mother.

Joining the ministry they really loved sounded like a dream come true for them, but it would have torn Dad away from his preteen son. To their credit, the couple decided not to make the move. Were they giving up a good opportunity? Sure they were. But they chose the best ministry they could be involved in: remaining close to the husband's son so he could raise him to be a man.

Lord, make me sensitive to my kids' needs, giving them priority over my personal wishes and desires. Give me discernment to know when I need to make hard choices for their well-being.

My Mom Is Dating Again!

R on, I never thought I'd say this, but my sixty-seven-year-old mom has a new boyfriend."

I'm hearing comments like that from lots of adult children these days. And it's strange for them. Maybe the thought of their parent dating again has crossed their mind before, but once it becomes a reality, it's just bizarre. Sometimes the child even becomes the coach, telling their parent how to ask for a date, or how to guard against sexual temptation. Weird.

When a parent reenters the dating scene, it can be a stressful time for everyone. Whether the child is ten or forty, they probably feel concerned about how the family will change—once again. They may be anxious, wondering how their mom's dating will affect their dad. And what will Christmas be like for extended family and grandkids?

Yes, old wounds will be reopened. There will be lots of questions to answer. So neither generation should make assumptions about how the other will cope. It may be two people who are dating, but this is a family matter. And you need to talk.

Father, when new relationships affect our family, help us be open
about our concerns and generous in our trust of each other.

Sitting on a Hot Stove

Mark Twain once said, "A cat that sits on a hot stove lid won't sit on a hot stove lid again." And then he added, "Neither will it sit on a cold one." When the death of a spouse or a divorce precedes a stepfamily marriage, it's easy for spouses to fear getting burned again. The problem is, the fear of getting hurt again makes us tend to withhold ourselves. We stop doing the things that love would normally prompt us to do, making it more likely that something will go wrong.

Well, that tendency is obviously not going to help our relationship, so what's the antidote to falling victim to a self-fulfilling prophecy? Simply this: Love as if you've never been burned before. That's definitely going to take some prayer and a whole lot of courage. But just think of the rewards that will come when you do unto your spouse as you would have them do unto you.

God, please help me break free from any residual negative effects from past relationships that keep me from loving fully and freely in the present.

Speak the Truth in Love

When a relationship seems fragile, it's tempting to stop speaking the truth. New friendships, new marriages, and new stepfamilies all lead to the same temptation: to avoid saying the hard thing and to sidestep the truth. Why? Because the relationship feels delicate and frail—you're not sure if it's strong enough to handle the truth.

Yes, we have to be sensitive to the relationship, but sugarcoating our response tends to backfire and just create resentment. Ephesians 4 says we should put away falsehood and speak truth to each other. It explains that we can even be angry without sinning if we learn to manage the anger so it doesn't corrupt the conversation and dictate our behavior (vv. 25–26).

So in your home, instead of walking on eggshells, share your thoughts and feelings in a healthy, collaborative manner. You just might discover that those shells are not as brittle as you think.

Father, help us create a family environment where every person feels secure in sharing their thoughts and feelings in a respectful way, even when it's necessary to say things that are hard for others to hear.

Avoid Unhealthy Coalitions

Are there any unhealthy coalitions going on in your home? Partnerships or coalitions in the business world often help two companies accomplish their goals. In families, coalitions can be either helpful or destructive, depending on who's involved. A healthy coalition between Mom and Dad creates a strong parenting system that supports children as they grow. But an unhealthy coalition between a parent and child—against the other parent—sabotages the authority of *both* parents and teaches children to manipulate other people.

Single-parent families and stepfamilies are highly susceptible to this dangerous dynamic. In stepfamilies, it's easy for the biological parent and their child to join ranks, so to speak, against the stepparent. But this nearly always creates conflict for the child and stepparent and sabotages the marriage.

Hey, it's great to be close to your child, but when you team up with them against someone else, everyone ends up losing.

Help us always be on guard against the development of any unhealthy alliances that divide loyalties and weaken the unity of our marriage and family.

June 14

Disconnect to Stay Connected

The game hide-and-seek was a lot of fun as a kid, wasn't it? But when it comes to adult relationships, this game is no fun at all. For example, have you ever had a friend just disappear on you because they were in love? They went bonkers over some new person and you became an afterthought. That's not much fun, is it?

Today's technology allows us to run off in an instant and hide from those we love. One spouse disappears into Facebook, while the other checks work email "just one more time" before bed. Your family sits down for dinner but then begins to text other people while ignoring one another—everybody's hiding, but nobody's doing the seeking.

Let's get disciplined, folks. Make yourself available to the ones you care most about. Unhook. Detach. Sign out and log off. Don't play hide-and-seek with the people you love! Instead, work to be found by them.

Lord, help us break free from the addiction to gadgets and technology and instead give top priority to staying personally connected with our loved ones.

Make Her More

Did Jesus' love and sacrifice for us make us *more* or *less*? The answer is pretty obvious: It made us more. Ephesians 5:25–27 says that Christ's love for us, the church, made us sanctified, cleansed, and without spot or wrinkle or blemish so he can present us "in splendor." Now we are holy and blameless through his sacrifice on our behalf. Wow, that's definitely a whole lot more!

Now, here's the message for men in this passage: God calls us to love our wives just like that. Because of how you love her, she should be more, not less. A selfish, controlling, critical, inattentive husband makes his wife less. But a thoughtful, kind, encouraging, considerate husband makes her more. More of what God has called and gifted her to be.

"Husbands, love your wives, as Christ loved the church and gave himself up for her" . . . to make her *more* (Ephesians 5:25).

Lord Jesus, I want to learn how to give my wife the same love you modeled when you sacrificed yourself for me. May my words and behavior build her up to become the person you created her to be.

Show Some Respect

The song "Respect" may have been made famous by soul singer Aretha Franklin, but the lyrics were written by a man.

You know, ladies, it may be true that the quickest way to a man's heart is through his stomach, but the best way to *keep* his heart is by offering him your respect. To a man, respect communicates admiration and appreciation. Both of which, to a man, spell *love*.

That's why the apostle Paul, in Ephesians 5, summarizes his treatise on marriage by encouraging women not to *love* their mates—as he specifically instructs the husbands—but to *respect* them (v. 33). So find a way today to express respect to your husband. Thank him for providing for your family. Tell him how much you appreciate his faithfulness to your marriage. Or if you're the stepmom to his kids, compliment them and his parenting of them.

R-E-S-P-E-C-T. Now you know what it means to him. So go ahead and sock it to him!

Father, help us live out your design for marriage by loving each other unconditionally and always treating each other with appreciation and respect.

Celebrate Father's Day

Last month we all celebrated Mother's Day, and now I'm wondering: What do you have planned for Father's Day? I have to admit right off the bat that today's thought might be a little self-serving. I am a dad, after all, and hey, I do enjoy being in the spotlight on Father's Day.

It's interesting that one poll showed that most people feel that moms get more attention on Mother's Day than dads receive on Father's Day. I wonder why that is? *And* I wonder if stepdads get as much attention as biological fathers do.

The good news is that we men aren't that complicated. Know what would really mean a lot to us on Father's Day? Just a few simple words: "Dad, I appreciate you for . . ." Finish that sentence and I promise you will make our day. We can run on that for—oh, about a year.

Lord, thank you for my husband's faithfulness to our family. Help me and our children show him how much we love and value him as a spouse, a father, and a friend.

Don't Buy the Lie

Dad, whatever you do, don't buy the lie.

The Father of Lies is a master at deception. Satan tells a lot of lies—all with the intent of destroying what God has designed and breaking our relationship with him. I find that men are especially vulnerable to the lie that they don't matter much in their children's lives. That's why so many fathers walk away from their kids, but so few mothers do.

Stepfathers who also have biological children have an added pressure: guilt. If you spend more time with your stepchildren than your own children, guilt and the lie that you don't matter makes some dads disconnect from their own kids. *They're better off with me out of the way*, they think. Other men go the opposite direction and remain distant from their stepchildren even though they live in the same home. Both approaches come at the expense of the kids.

So hear this loud and clear: Dad, you are important. Please don't be tempted to buy the lie.

Heavenly Father, strengthen me to see the significance of my role in the lives of my children and stepchildren. Help me to be the person they need me to be.

Just Say What You Need

Are you interested in stronger relationships? Here's a tip: Gently say what you need. We all have needs in relationships. But instead of actually expressing the need, too often we beat around the bush. A spouse will barrage their mate with an avalanche of words, but never simply say, "I need more time with you." A teenager will stay out late, break a few rules, and be obstinate instead of telling their parents, "I don't like who I am; I need more encouragement from you." Or a stepparent who feels rejected by a stepchild might withdraw from them instead of admitting that they feel awkward and want to find a way to get along.

Yes, being direct and transparent can be tough. It can leave you feeling vulnerable and at risk of being hurt. But getting to the point makes connection with that other person far more likely to happen. It also increases the chances that the needs of everyone in the family will be met.

Lord, help each person in our family find the courage to be transparent about their own needs and the sensitivity to respond to each other's needs with gentleness and respect.

Bear One Another's Burdens

A ccording to Galatians 6, each of us is required to carry our own responsibilities (v. 5). But sometimes the weight feels like more than we can handle. God has the answer for that. He tells us, "Bear one another's burdens" (v. 2). In other words, when your load seems too heavy for you to bear, I'm supposed to help you out. And vice versa.

Of course, there are many different kinds of burdens: financial stress, struggling relationships, disasters, and illness, just to name a few. A common one in stepfamilies is grief for lost or broken relationships. Nearly everyone is carrying their own grief, plus the family has a collective grief to bear. But even then you can be a resource to one another.

When you pray for your family, ask God to clothe family members with compassion and empathy for the losses and sadness of others. Pray for patience and the willingness to support one another and to bear the burdens of others as the family grows together.

Father, give each member of our family the desire and under-standing of how to help carry the burdens of the others.

Take Care of Yourself

Is self-care the same thing as selfishness? The Christian faith urges us to deny ourselves and to serve others. Jesus taught that being great in God's eyes means putting others first and being a servant to all. But does that indicate that all self-care is selfish? I don't think so.

Mark 1 tells us that after healing many people and attracting a huge crowd, Jesus disappeared the next morning. Just imagine the lines of people who had spent the night waiting for Jesus, and now the disciples can't find him. Turns out he went off by himself to pray. I think that's a good example of self-care. And when pressured to go back to the crowds, he said the better option was to go preach somewhere else. That sounds like self-care, too.

Maybe the kind of self-care that orients you toward the purposes of God and prepares you to serve others isn't selfishness at all. As a matter of fact, it's quite the opposite.

Father, help us learn self-care that meets our physical, emotional, and spiritual needs and equips us to better serve our family and those around us.

June 22

Choose Your Set of Problems

When you select a mate, you are also choosing a set of problems—for the rest of your life! It turns out that nearly 70 percent of the conflicts couples face are about perpetual issues, in other words, disagreements they can't seem to resolve. And many of those issues are rooted in personality differences—things that likely won't change. For example, if the husband is an extrovert and the wife wishes he didn't have to be with people all the time.

Stepcouples also find they married themselves to perpetual problems they didn't anticipate. Like ongoing conflict between homes, or financial troubles, or an *ex*-mother-in-law. You may not have seen that one coming, but it's now a part of your life.

Yes, to get married means to marry yourself to a certain set of hassles. The quicker you accept it and ask God for the humility and patience to adjust to it, the better off you'll be.

Lord, I ask for wisdom, humility, and grace to deal with all the annoyances and conflicts I willingly accepted when I married my spouse.

Step-Wedding

When strong winds blow, you need an anchor to hold you steady. And this doesn't apply only to ocean voyages. Sometimes at a blended family wedding, you can stand back and watch the winds of confusion blow. Tension in stepfamily relationships makes people guarded and anxious, even as they plaster on smiles for the sake of the bride and groom.

The groom's side is not sure what to do with the bride's side, and vice versa. The poor wedding coordinator struggles with who is related to whom and has no idea which labels to use. But if you look closely, you can see it. Right there, in the middle of the blustery winds, the bride and groom—and the vows that tie them together—become an anchor in the storm.

Anchored to each other and to God, the couple in turn serves as an anchor for their extended family. Just the way God intended.

As we stay closely moored to you and to each other, help our relationship serve as a stabilizing influence for our children and for both our families.

How to Cook a Stepfamily

How *do* you cook a stepfamily? Stepfamilies are sometimes called "blended" families, so you must prepare them with a blender, right? Actually, no. Because blenders are really rough on ingredients. They chop them up and force them to combine with other ingredients. Stepparents do the very same thing whenever they make kids feel guilty because they don't call a stepdad Daddy or they don't want to hang out with their stepsiblings. Unfortunately, the blender method is not a good idea for combining families.

No, you're much better off cooking your stepfamily with a Crockpot.[19] You know: the slowwwww and easy method. Be patient with the ingredients of your family, letting each person combine with others at their own pace, in their own way. They'll feel less pressure, and you'll enjoy the process a whole lot more. Most important, the finished product will be a masterpiece.

Lord, grant us patience as we wait for our family members to blend together in their own time. Remind us not to force unrealistic expectations on each other.

Try this: If you haven't done it already, try the family activity on a related theme found on February 9. Good family fun!

Make a Promise

Did you know that sometimes at your wedding, it's appropriate to express vows to someone in addition to your groom or bride? Maybe you saw the online video that went viral and touched so many hearts. It shows a groom expressing vows to his bride, *and* to her daughter. You see, this stepdad-to-be knew that marrying a single parent means accepting the package deal—which in this case included a young girl.

This man promised to play games with her, to protect and love her, and to teach her how to say her prayers. He vowed to show her how a man should treat a woman by the way he treated her mother.

Now, this little girl might not have known how to return the commitment to him at that point in her life. But one thing she knew right from the start: Her stepdad was deeply committed to her.

Father, I never want my kids or stepkids to doubt my devotion and commitment. Give me the right words to express my promise to do all I can for them, and the courage to speak those words.

Put Others First

L et me ask you a question: Has your desire to be central in someone's life ever caused you to be harsh or unfair toward somebody else? Maybe you heard about the letter that Candice Curry wrote to her daughter's stepmom, Ashley. Candice admitted that, wanting to be central in her daughter's life, at first she'd hoped Ashley would be a "terrible beast" so her daughter would not be able to respect or relate to her.

But then Candice chose to set aside her selfish need to compete, admitted that Ashley was an asset to her daughter, and buried the hatchet. Her daughter, Stiles, got a mom plus a bonus mom who live in peace. The letter went viral and caught the attention of the national media.[20] Why? Because the courage to put others first is rare in our culture.

Sometimes for love to win, we have to stop trying to be the center of someone's life and just be a servant instead.

Lord, cleanse me from any selfish, egotistical desire that might lead me to put down another person in order to build myself up.

Get a Couple Checkup

Would you let your car go 100,000 miles before getting an oil change? Would you go twenty-five years without a dental checkup? I seriously doubt it. If you do, you're probably going to pay the price in the long run. Getting a checkup is one of the smartest things you can do for the care and maintenance of what matters to you. Yet married couples rarely, if ever, get a checkup on their relationship.

The online Couple Checkup is an easy-to-use relationship inventory that helps you discover your strengths and identify areas that represent vulnerability. It even tailors itself to whether you are dating, engaged, married, or in a blended family. The reason we get dental checkups is to prevent pain in the future. And doesn't that also sound like a good reason to get a *couple* checkup now?

Take the Couple Checkup at SmartStepfamilies.com. (The books *The Smart Stepfamily Marriage* [Ron Deal and David Olson] and *Dating and the Single Parent* [Ron Deal] include a code to get a discount on the Couple Checkup.)

Lord, we commit before you to invest the time, attention, and energy required to help our marriage stay strong and flourish.

That's Just How I Feel

I can't help it. That's just how I feel."

As a counselor I've heard those words—and that excuse—countless times. "I know it's not pretty, but I can't help how I feel." But according to the Bible, how we behave should be determined by what we think and believe, not how we're feeling at the moment. And the best source to shape our thinking is God's wisdom found in his Word.

Romans 12:2 tells us to "be transformed by the renewal of your mind"; then we will know "what is good and acceptable and perfect" in God's eyes. Mistreating someone because they hurt you first is driven by a feeling. Engaging in porn, bad-mouthing family members, resenting your ex-spouse—those are all motivated by feelings, too. They're certainly not based on God's truths.

Do you want a stronger family? Then let God's wisdom determine how you act, not your changeable emotions.

Father God, transform my thinking according to your Word so that my behavior always reflects your truth, regardless of how I am feeling at any given moment.

When Anger Isn't Really Anger

People who love well know what to ignore and what to follow up on. I know it's completely upside down, but when someone who cares for you is angry, it's as if they're saying, "I need you." Here's how it works: When we feel unimportant to someone we value—a parent, a spouse, a family member—we get angry to hide our feelings of vulnerability. Anger on the outside may actually be covering up fear and a desire to be important.

Now, what mature spouses, parents, and stepparents do when receiving someone's anger is look past it to the desire behind it. Instead of anger or disappointment they hear, "I need you and want to be closer. . . . I miss you." And they move toward that desire. They may calmly listen and give space for the anger or they may say something like "Your anger tells me you wish you could trust me more." Whatever the response, they hear the invitation for further connection and they move toward it. And that's when emotional pain dissolves into peace.

Lord God, help me remember to look past a loved one's anger to see what it is they need from me.

June 30

Remember Your Vows

F or better or for worse, till death do us part."

I heard these familiar words when I attended a wedding the other day. I've decided that it would be a good idea for every married person to attend a friend or family member's wedding from time to time. Why? Because the wedding ceremony reminds you of what you once promised; it helps you remember the heart you had for your mate on the day you said, "I do." And because, sadly, life has a way of diluting and discoloring that day, but a wedding takes you back and refreshes those special memories.

Think for a moment about your vow to protect and honor one another. You promised to leave behind former loyalties and to cleave to each other. To sustain, as your ring symbolizes, a never-ending commitment. To make your marriage a statement about how God loves, desires, and pursues us. And to make oneness a top priority, till death do you part. That is worth remembering and the vow worth refreshing.

Father, we stand before you as one, renewing our promise to live each day as a flesh-and-blood illustration of your unconditional love and faithfulness.

A Cycle of Love and Grace

Jesus came to turn spiritual outsiders into insiders. Like the shepherd desperately searching for the one lost sheep in Matthew 18, Jesus sought out the disenfranchised, the unwelcomed, and the lost. Now, what's really cool is watching people experience that love and grace for themselves and then extend it to others in turn.

I've seen this played out in blended families over and over. A child abandoned by a parent begins to bloom under the loving care of a step-parent. A mother speaks well of her children's stepmother and insists they respect her when in her home.

See what's happening in these scenarios? Gratitude to God for his hand of mercy is pouring itself out in the form of love and grace toward others. And this is how we change the world: experiencing his love, and then extending grace to someone else.

Jesus, thank you for seeking me when I was an outsider and for drawing me into your fold. Now help me learn to reach out to others with that same gracious love and acceptance.

Kids in Two Homes

Two-thirds of stepparents also have biological children of their own. You know, one common struggle we parents have is balancing our demands: work, taking care of our home, time invested in our marriage and kids, and perhaps caring for aging parents. It really stretches us. Well, what if you have children in two different homes? Stepkids in one and biological children in another? That will stretch you even more.

Here's a tip: Try your best to fully engage with whomever you're with. In your heart you might be divided, but you can only be in one place at a time. So accept that reality and choose to be in the present moment. Then take advantage of small moments to connect with kids in the other home. Remember that a simple text or video call can help keep you in touch across the distance.

Yes, it's difficult to balance your parenting this way; some days you may feel torn in two. But when you feel stretched too thin, remember to stay flexible by grabbing whatever opportunity comes your way to love those kids.

Lord, help me treasure the time I spend with each of my kids, always giving them my full attention.

July 3

Build a Solid Foundation

When you're ready to marry someone, you have full confidence that the relationship is built on a solid foundation. But please don't try to build that confidence by living together. Unmarried couples who live together imagine that they are somehow taking a step forward, when really they are merely pretending to be serious. The research is clear: Despite what cohabiting couples feel about their relationship, objectively they have lower levels of commitment, higher breakup rates, and sadly, for those that do go on to marry—higher rates of divorce.[21]

Cohabiting doesn't help you know if you're really ready to get married any more than dipping your toe in the shallow end helps you know whether or not you can swim. So take God at his Word and trust that he wants the best for you. Keep your objectivity by not cohabiting and by saving sex until marriage. That way, your confidence will grow for the right reasons and you'll make solid decisions for your future.

Trusting that you have my best interests at heart, I commit to following the guidelines for healthy relationships that you have laid down in your Word.

Celebrate the Light

Have you ever watched fireworks—on a sunny day? No, of course, you haven't. That would be pretty boring, wouldn't it? Fireworks are made for nighttime because the dark sky provides the perfect backdrop for the glorious displays of colors and lights.

You know, some of us have a dark backdrop to our lives. We've experienced great loss, disappointment, financial strain, uncertainty—times when we didn't know how we were going to make it. Or maybe we've suffered from brokenness in a relationship or family. Maybe you're even going through something like that right now.

Like fireworks, God has a way of lighting up the dark sky. Unfortunately, the darkness remains. But the light draws your attention away from the dark and offers a different perspective that is bright and hopeful. So, while you watch the fireworks on this Fourth of July, rest assured that God has not forgotten you. And remember that compared to your darkness, he is light—a spectacular light!

Lord, use the dark days in my life to highlight the dazzling brightness of your love, power, and mercy.

July 5

No More Shame

In the Lord's Prayer, Jesus taught us to seek forgiveness for our debts. But even after asking for forgiveness, do you sometimes still feel indebted?

The parents in one newly blended family poured out their hearts to me. Sin had caused their previous divorces and they felt dirty before the Lord. I reminded them that Romans 5 tells us that Christ died for the ungodly (v. 6), and that we can have peace with God when we come to him in faith (v. 1).

Yes, shame is really hard to shake sometimes. And false guilt is one of Satan's favorite tools to use against us. It blocks our communion with God, stunts our spiritual growth, and makes us miserable. One antidote is to memorize Romans 8:1: "There is therefore now no condemnation for those who are in Christ Jesus."

Whenever you experience false guilt, pray this for your family: "Lord, may we feel the warmth of your love and acceptance. If we feel shame for past sin, may it be washed away by your grace. Let us stand confidently in your mercy, not feeling second-class or unworthy, but forgiven and loved."

Unlearn and Learn

Did you know that in order to be a loving spouse, sometimes you have to *unlearn* what you've already learned? Learning to live with the preferences and quirks of your spouse is one way to become a great partner. Learning that your wife is not a morning person and that you shouldn't speak to her until after her third cup of coffee might be just one of hundreds of little lessons you need to learn.

But sometimes you have to unlearn what you've learned in the past. Sabrina, who was tragically widowed with two young children, discovered after getting remarried that her second husband didn't like his back scratched. She also learned that when he was quiet, it didn't mean he felt unhappy; it meant he was content.[22]

You see, if you don't unlearn what you learned before, you can make the wrong assumption. So stop assuming and start listening. After all, you have a lot to learn.

Father, help me unlearn what is no longer helpful and learn whatever I need to know in order to be a blessing to my spouse.

Let Reality Be the Teacher

think we can all agree that while parenting is rewarding, it sure is tough work. So let me suggest that whenever possible, get out of the way. What I mean is, whenever it's appropriate, let reality be the teacher for your child or stepchild. I recently learned that you cannot park your car after 4:00 p.m. along the National Mall in Washington, DC. Do you know how I learned that? I got a ticket for doing it.

Hey, I know we want to prevent our children from ever experiencing distress or inconvenience. But when we protect them from the natural consequences of their choices or behavior, we steal their opportunity to learn lessons that really stick with them for the long haul. If they forget to set an alarm, they're late for work. If they don't start a school project till the last minute, it's not your deadline to meet. Just get out of the way and let life teach them lessons they need to learn.

Lord, never let my desire to protect my children keep them from learning life lessons about the natural consequences of their actions.

Bumpy Transitions

D ad, I just want you to be happy."

That was exactly what Dan wanted to hear. A widower who had fallen in love again, he had just asked his twenty-nine-year-old son how he felt about Cheryl. Eric's first response to the new relationship was very positive. But later on he grew resentful, jealous, and even angry.

Of course, not all adult children feel this way, but it's not uncommon either. They struggle sometimes just like younger kids do. If you're a parent in this situation, a little understanding can really help. This transition is a lot harder for them than it is for you, so be patient and willing to wait for their acceptance if you have to.

If you're the adult child, get in touch with your fears and pray about them. Some of your concerns may need to be openly addressed. But others, quite honestly, just need to be let go. Ask God to help you decide which is which.

Help me accept each new family member you bring into our circle, trusting you for wisdom to recognize when to bring up concerns that need to be discussed.

Blended Math

It's time for a little stepfamily math.[23] Let's see, a biological family of five has twenty relationships to manage. But a stepfamily of five has a lot more. You have to add their ex-spouses, their new partners, the new partner's children, and any baby born to the new couple (for simplicity's sake we'll leave out extended family). So really, a stepfamily of five has 210 relationships to manage.

Oh, and then there's the Confused Identity Multiplier. You see, the step-parent has one idea of what his or her role is in the family. The biological parent has a second opinion. The stepchildren and biological child have others—even the spouse's ex has expectations of their role. In one scenario that calculates to 420 relationships. No wonder stepfamilies are tired!

You can't control all of those relationships, so make sure you manage your marriage and give each other a little TLC. Together you can stand against the numbers.

Lord, despite the confusion and complexity of functioning as a stepfamily, we trust in your guidance to help us focus on the simplicity of loving and respecting each other.

Call for Help

In just one year, home fires in the United States accounted for close to 16,000 injuries and more than 3,200 deaths. But there's a home fire of a different kind that is just as destructive.

I assume we can all agree that there are no perfect families, right? And while we all know that our own family is not perfect, sometimes we think other families are. Well, you can be sure that no matter how they look to outsiders, those other families are flawed just as yours is.

Even while I write this material, my wife and I are working through a tiff we had this past weekend. Hey, everybody has a little house fire from time to time. But if there's a family conflict that can't be contained, there's no shame in calling the fire department. You know—a pastor or counselor or ministry that can offer assistance.

So if you find that things have heated up too much, don't stand there and watch the house burn down. Call for help.

Holy Spirit, give us discernment to recognize when family problems get to the point that we need to seek outside help.

Our True Destination

Remember those kindergarten field trips? To keep you from getting lost, the teachers would put each chaperone with a small group of kids, and sometimes they paired you up with a buddy. The idea was for the two of you to hold hands and keep each other safe. Well, in the field trip of life, God has grouped us with others, too; we call it the church. And some people are paired with a buddy; we call that marriage.

We need to understand that life is not the destination—heaven is. And the only marriage in heaven is between us and the Lord (see Matthew 22:30). Single people need this perspective so they won't over-value getting married. Dating people need it so they will only date believers. Married people need to remember it so they won't idolize one another, and remarried people so they won't worry whether they were the first love or the second.

Just imagine how much better our relationships will be if we focus on helping each other reach our true destination.

Help me see each relationship in my life from the viewpoint of eternity, making choices that help lead others to their ultimate destination of knowing you personally.

Sometimes It's Okay to Be Stubborn

When it comes to parenting, sometimes adults should be—well, stubborn! Let's be honest and admit that kids go through seasons of life when they can be downright prickly. Whether it's the terrible twos or the adolescent years, sometimes they're just tough to parent.

Stepparenting can have its challenging seasons as well. But what helps move both child and adult through these difficult times is a stepparent who persistently pursues relationship with the child and works toward resolution of any problematic issues. They are too stubborn to give up and too tenacious to give in.

You may have to seek support from outside resources or mentors, but at the end of the day . . . don't give up. Do you know what God is to us? A stubborn, loving presence who declares, "I will not leave you or forsake you" (Joshua 1:5; Hebrews 13:5). Be that for your kids and just see if stubborn love doesn't eventually win them over.

Father, thank you for never giving up on me in the past and for promising to stay with me in the future. Help me love my kids with that same stubborn love, even during the most difficult times.

Earn the Right to Lead

A stepparent can be a powerful influence in a child's life—as long as that stepparent is trusted. We all know how moms and dads can influence children. Over time they teach independent thinking and respect for rules. Their love fosters self-confidence and maturity. A stepparent can have this same influence, but they'll never get the chance if early on they're bossy, demanding, or inconsiderate. Act that way and the child will just pull away—and stay away.

Remember that they don't *have* to trust you; of course, you want them to, but they don't have to. So right from the beginning, work to build a relationship with the child at a pace they can accept. They've got their own life story that will influence how quickly and how fully they open up to you. Get to know it and respect it.

You earn the right to lead a child by being trustworthy, kind, and considerate. So focus on representing God's love and you'll become a powerful influence in their life.

Heavenly Father, I want to parent my children as you parent me: loving them unconditionally, guiding gently but firmly, and drawing them in with irresistible grace and kindness.

Stepgrandparents: A Vital Resource

America—and your family—has an endless energy resource, and it's not oil, gas, or solar energy. If you're feeling stumped, that's because you're probably thinking about the wrong kind of energy. I'm referring to the life energy that comes from being loved. And the underestimated resource that supplies it? Grandparents! Grandparents give us a safe place to belong while teaching life lessons from time to time, offering unconditional hugs, cooking wonderful meals, or taking us fishing. Grandparents are important.

And they're valuable to blended families, too. Whether it's reaching out to new family members and helping them feel like they belong, or asking parents how they can support their marriage and family, grandparents have an underestimated ability to create connections. To foster a safe place for children and nurture them. To offer love and acceptance, thereby infusing the family with a sense of joy and energy.

How are you inviting the grandparents in your stepfamily to be a resource?

Give us ideas about how to draw grandparents closer within our family circle so we can bless them even as we benefit from their maturity, wisdom, and love.

Keep Doing Good Anyway

Have you ever heard the expression "No good deed goes unpunished"? Boy, there's a lot of truth in that—for parents! It really is odd. You'd think that whenever someone extends kindness or does the right thing, they'd get a positive response in return. And I guess, generally speaking, they usually do. But often there's someone who responds negatively rather than showing gratitude.

Parents really need to be prepared for this. When you hold your kids accountable for their behavior, they won't praise your parenting skills; they'll probably balk and whine about it. When you make sacrifices to buy things for your child, they may take your selflessness for granted.

Stepparents really need to be reminded that some of what they do on behalf of children who are not their own will be unappreciated. But here's the good news: Even if they never respond, your Father who sees in secret promises to reward you (see Matthew 6:4).

Lord, help us stay committed to doing what's best for our children whether or not they express gratitude for our efforts and dedication.

Stepfamily Pros and Cons

I see you judging me because my family isn't 'normal.'. . . [But just like you] I didn't choose my family."

Kaleigh, a teenager, posted online about the pros and cons of growing up in a blended family. The cons: watching one parent be saddened by the behavior of the other, having to pack up her belongings and switch houses every week, losing some of her parents' attention to strange new family members. And the awareness that every unwanted change is changing her.

But Kaleigh acknowledged a couple of pros as well: the presence of not just two supportive parents, but four, and having a variety of siblings and relationships that bring new love into her life and help her to become a more well-rounded person. Yes, living in a stepfamily certainly has its pros and cons. But that just means you need God's love and guidance—like all families do.

Father, help us appreciate all the positive things our blended family brings into our lives and do everything we can to minimize the negative effects.

Create a Level Playing Field

Have you ever had someone treat your child unfairly? And did the hair on the back of your neck stand up like mine did? Boy, nothing riles a parent's protectiveness like their child being mistreated. But what if it's coming from your spouse?

Maya wrote to me complaining that her husband disciplines her kids more harshly than he disciplines his own. Plus, her kids have to do chores that his don't. Her kids are resentful, and Maya has grown defensive and hurt about the unfair treatment.

Without question, stepparents, you must strive to be equitable in your home. Generally speaking, everyone should be treated the same and held to the same standards. Yes, appropriating your time, money, and energy should take into consideration the age and maturity of each child, but there should be a level playing field. So do your best to be evenhanded—with liberty and justice for all!

Lord, help us treat each of our children with fairness and equality. When a situation arises that might seem unfair in the kids' eyes, remind us to be open about giving the reasons for our decision.

When Conflict Is a Good Thing

Would it surprise you to learn that compared to full or half-siblings, stepsiblings have *less* conflict? But it turns out, that may not be as good as it sounds.

All parents expect a little sibling conflict, but mostly we just want our kids to get along. Parents in stepfamilies want peace as well, and they normally take absence of conflict as a sign that the kids are accepting each other. They assume that the family is coming together smoothly. Because whenever conflict is present, the family feels divided.

Now here's what's ironic: The reason that stepsiblings are less negative and have more positive communication might be because they feel *less* like family. In other words, feeling safe and connected frees siblings to be more honest about negative emotions and differing opinions. That means the more bonded stepsiblings grow over time, the more conflict you can expect to erupt.

So in some cases, more conflict would be wonderful. . . . I think.

Help us create an environment where family members feel free to express their honest opinions and emotions, and then grace-fully accept the conflict that naturally comes with that bonding process.

The Ghost
of Marriage Past

Is there any chance you are haunted by "The Ghost of Marriage Past"? Don discovered that he was. His first wife had been reckless with money, maxing out their credit cards and continually lying to him about it. The first time his second wife, Judy, forgot to tell him about a bill, Don starting sweating bullets. He completely overreacted to Judy's innocent mistake. You see, Don is being haunted by the ghost of marriage past. And if he doesn't become a ghost buster, he just might end up sabotaging his present marriage.

I urge you to take some time to reflect, look in the mirror, and see if there's a ghost hovering over your shoulder. And if there is, pray about it, share it with your spouse, and then visit us at FamilyLife Blended (FamilyLife.com/blended). We want to help you bust free from what may be haunting you.

Father, please reveal to me any way that my past relationships threaten my marriage and family life. And do the same for my spouse. Help us share with each other what we need to discuss, and lead us to any resources we need to break free.

Different Degrees of Love

Friends. Some of us have a lot of them and some of us have a few. But do you love them all the same? No, of course you don't love all your friends *exactly* the same. Some are closer than others; some you just barely know, although someday they might become your BFF.

Family members are kind of like that. You may have lots of siblings, but there's one you're closer to than the others. Or you know one set of grandparents much better than the other. And then there's that weird uncle you never see except at family reunions.

It's interesting that I sometimes hear members of blended families admit that they love one another to differing degrees—and they feel guilty about it. I'm not sure why. We all have family that we love to differing degrees. But the important thing is, they are still family.

Lord, take away any false guilt we feel about being closer to some family members than others. Let us focus not on the degree of love we feel, but the commitment that binds us all together.

When Love Is Not So Easy

Have you ever started into a project and then discovered that it was more difficult than you had anticipated? Sometimes, marriage and family are just like that. Danny had no idea how hard it would be to love his wife. "She has so many emotional scars from her past," he told me. "We've been together for nine years and I'm still trying to find a way around her insecurities."

Maybe you've also felt frustrated trying to love someone while having no idea how to help them heal their scars. I certainly don't think there is a one-size-fits-all solution for dealing with this, but I do believe that a stubborn grace and steadfast love are two things that seem to overcome a lot. After all, isn't that how Jesus works in our lives?

So don't be easily defeated by the scars of those you love. Rise above, and just keep on loving them.

Heavenly Father, when it comes to loving someone whose insecurities and emotional scars get in the way, help me be stubborn and steadfast like you.

Earn Their Trust While Waiting for Their Love

Stepparents, don't just aim for love from your stepkids—work to earn their trust.

To have a healthy relationship with someone it really takes both love *and* trust. If you love someone but don't fully trust them, you're always going to be cautious. If you trust them but don't love them, you'll only allow yourself to get so close to them before pulling away.

Now, with many adopted, foster, and stepkids, trust eventually opens the door to love. So I encourage you to build trust by being someone who's emotionally and physically safe to be around. Show them that you're committed to them—that you'll never leave them, no matter what. And demonstrate that you love them even on their worst days.

Show them that your *yes* means yes and your *no* means just that. Be a person they can trust, and it's much more likely that you'll be a person they can love.

Father, help me resist the temptation to try to force my stepkids to love me. Grow me into the kind of person they can trust and feel safe around.

The Blame Game

Ever since Adam and Eve, people have been playing the blame game. We all know how to play it, don't we? Something's not right in the world, so we find someone to blame. And when there's conflict in a relationship, we blame the other person for their part while conveniently ignoring our own contribution.

Blended families do this, too. Biological parents blame the stepparent. Stepparents might blame the children, or the parent in the other home. The other home blames the ex-spouse. The mother-in-law blames the new son- or daughter-in-law. And round and round it goes. . . .

Jesus said, "First take the log out of your own eye, and then you will see clearly to take the speck out of your brother's eye" (Matthew 7:5). Focusing on your part of the interaction astronomically improves the odds that you can change the situation. So why not skip your turn in the blame game and take a long, honest look in the mirror instead?[24]

Lord, I hereby quit the blame game. Help me resist the temptation to automatically blame others when a problem arises. Instead, I will first examine my own behavior to see what part I've played.

Helping a Troubled Heart, Part 1

Troubled emotions in our kids trouble us as parents, don't they? There are plenty of things that can trouble our kids: friends, grades, family struggles, finding their place in the world. And as their parents, we don't like to see them hurting. That's one reason we're sometimes tempted to minimize their troubled emotions. "I'm sure she didn't mean it." "Don't worry about missing the ball; it's only a game." We make comments like that and then wonder why they didn't seem to help the situation.

Let's stop and think about what's happening here: We're trying to talk our child out of feeling bad. But does that work with you? I didn't think so. So try taking a different approach to help them sort through their emotions. Calm *yourself* as you listen, so you'll be better able to calm *them*. Acknowledge their concerns. Then pray with them and share a hug to show how concerned you are. After that, who knows—they might even let you give a little advice.

Teach me to respect my children by never minimizing or over-reacting to their negative feelings when they're troubled or upset about something.

Helping a Troubled Heart, Part 2

Parenting a troubled child always begins with managing ourselves first. If our child is sad, angry, or depressed—no matter what caused it—we will also experience an emotion. If we feel annoyed or aggravated with the child, our response to their negative emotions will likely be dismissive or sharp. If we're worried or anxious for them, we may try to fix ourselves by making them feel better. But here's the problem: Both of these responses are self-serving.

During conversations, always start out by noticing your own emotions and keeping them in check. Then you can listen better to your child and hear what's *behind* their words. For example, sadness says that something is missing. Anger often communicates, "I'm hurt" or "I'm frustrated." Feeling alone reflects a desire to belong. So if you want to help your troubled child, step away from your own emotions and focus on what their words are really communicating.

Lord, help me to never let my own feelings and attitudes keep me from truly hearing what my child is trying to tell me.

Go Ahead and Say It

Has anyone ever said this to you: "You know, I'm just getting to know you, but I really appreciate you. I'd like to get to know you better." A few times in my life, I've had someone essentially say those very words to me. And I don't know about you, but it makes me feel kind of good inside. And it opens me up to getting to know the person who said it. It encourages connection and helps move people from a superficial acquaintance toward a more solid relationship.

Foster parents and stepparents can express this same sentiment to a child. Kids like hearing that they are valued just as adults do. And feeling affirmed and appreciated opens their heart toward you. Now, be prepared—they may not instantly open up to you and be transparent. But that's okay. One of you has to step out in courage and take that first step toward building a bridge; it might as well be you.

Give me the courage to be the one who initiates relationship building by freely expressing my appreciation for loved ones and my desire to know them on a deeper level.

Round Off the Rough Edges

Let me ask you a question: Do you enjoy hanging out with people who are harsh, angry, and difficult to get along with? Yeah, me neither. I once asked a group of veteran stepparents for their best advice for other stepparents. The item at the top of their lists? Round off your rough edges.

This isn't exactly rocket science, after all. If you're naturally angry, critical, quick-tempered, controlling, or stubborn—then guess what? Don't expect your stepchildren to warm up to you or trust you. And don't expect your spouse to trust their kids with you either. I'm constantly amazed how some stepparents think that just because they're an adult, they can treat a child poorly—in ways they would never dream of treating a neighbor—and still expect the child to like and honor them.

No, if you want to be liked, then round off your rough edges and become more likable. And just watch how much more smoothly things go.

Father, make me aware of any rough edges that keep people from wanting to be around me. Shape me into the kind of person my spouse and kids can trust and like.

No Regrets

If your parenting came to an end today, would you have any regrets? Nan and I have three sons. In 2009 our middle son, Connor, died from an illness at the age of twelve. From my perspective, I certainly wasn't finished parenting him. But today I can honestly say that I don't have any regrets about the time we had together.

We went fishing. We laughed together and we traveled together. Our family celebrated his talents and gifts with him, and urged him to use those gifts to serve others. I worked hard to enter his world during a season when I didn't fully understand him. We talked about sexuality and other awkward subjects. Nan and I shared the gospel with him, and I'm so glad we did. Because for him, eternity came sooner than we expected.

Parents, we can't count on tomorrow. So love them today and parent them today. No regrets.

Heavenly Father, show us how to lead and love our family day by day so that each one of us is prepared to face eternity whenever it comes, and those left behind will have no regrets.

To learn more about the nonprofit ministry working with formerly trafficked children we started in Connor's memory, visit ConnorsSong.com.

Two Kinds of Love

I really appreciated Mike's honest words: "I just didn't realize how hard it would be to love my stepdaughter the same as my two kids." I respected Mike's candor about his struggle. In my experience, most stepparents who catch themselves having to work to develop and show affection for their stepkids feel really guilty about it. They make a conscious choice not to have favorites, and they do their best to treat each child equally. But even so, love does come more easily for some than for others.

Actually, I think what these parents are noticing is the difference between the deep natural affection and attachment parents instinctively feel toward their biological children, and the choosing type of love that grows over time toward adopted kids and stepchildren. Listen, both of these are love. They may have a different visceral experience on occasion, but *both* communicate value and worth to a child.

So Mike, keep going. Sounds like you're doing just fine.

Lord, take away any guilt about different levels of affection we feel toward our kids. Help us simply focus on making sure each child feels valued and cherished.

Stop the Tug-of-War

Have you ever been caught in a loyalty tug-of-war? Well, the odds are your kids have.

For young and adult children alike, feeling stuck between your parents—especially between your mom and stepmom—is a common experience. And that's a very uncomfortable place to be.

When family members pressure someone to spend more time at one house than the other, loyalties get divided. When a parent lays a guilt trip on kids for loving people in the other home, it backs them into a pressure-filled corner. The door to conflict and resentment is flung wide open. And guess who always loses out—the kids.

What kids really need is permission. Permission to like, love, and value everyone in their family—without cost. Without being forced to take sides. Instead of playing a selfish tug-of-war aimed at taking care of your own needs, drop the rope. And let love lead the way.

Father, I never want my kids to feel like they are caught in a tug-of-war. Help all our family relationships be so filled with love and grace that everyone knows they're on the same side.

Give Each Other Some Space

Depending on their visitation schedule, many kids have spent extended time at one home this summer; soon they will transition back to the other home for the beginning of the school year. This is another one of those occasions where people feel a little sad about leaving, glad about arriving, and perhaps a little confused about how to manage the transition.

There can be a lot of emotion bouncing around, so I urge you to give each other some breathing space at first. Parents, you may be eager to hear about your kids' summer, but sometimes they need a little adjustment time before they're ready to talk about it. And all of you need a little space to ease back into the household routine and to prepare for the new school year.

So cut each other some slack, talk it through when you're ready, and together you'll find your way.

Lord, remind us to be patient and understanding with each other as we go through different seasons. Help us begin preparing now for the new school year, covering every aspect in prayer.

Thirty Years to Gratitude

Sometimes I think we should give gold medals to stepparents. Why? Well, a man once told me that it took thirty years before he could tell his stepfather he loved him. Thirty years! I'm sure his stepfather struggled through those long years looking and longing for his stepson's love, acceptance, and gratitude. But despite his efforts, godly attitude, and leadership, his stepson just couldn't allow himself to express his love.

Now, I know that's an extreme example; thankfully, not all stepparents have to wait that long. But it is fairly common for them to have all the responsibilities of parenthood and receive very few of the rewards. And that's why they should receive a gold medal. Or at least a hug and a thank-you. From somebody. Maybe you.

Father, help me keep on loving and doing my best for my children even when I see no signs of appreciation or acknowledgment. May my goal be to hear you someday say to me, "Well done, good and faithful servant" (Matthew 25:21).

Bless Your Family with a Will

D o you know what *intestacy* is? No, it's not a stomach virus. It's when a court has to decide after you die who is entitled to receive your assets. You see, there's a whole body of laws that take over when you pass away without leaving a will. And statistics show that only 45 percent of Americans have a will.

Do you want family members fighting over your stuff? I don't think so. But you might inadvertently be setting them up for a lot of heartache if you don't have a will in place. Why would you put people you love in that situation? And for stepfamilies, why let the court give your spouse or their children things you wanted to give to your biological children? Instead, why not bless your family with *your* will?

> *Father, help us learn what we need to know about financial planning and take the appropriate steps to protect the best interests of every family member's future. Keep us from making any arrangements that would create disagreements, conflict, or resentment after one of us passes away.*

Be Prepared to Work

Hey, if your kids and I can't get along naturally then maybe we shouldn't have gotten together in the first place. It shouldn't have to be this much work."

Ever felt like that? Clearly this stepfather is frustrated. He's tried his best to connect with his stepchildren, but the door stays firmly shut. It's difficult—for him and for them—and now he's discouraged.

Actually, what's natural for new blended family relationships is for them to be awkward, fragile, and strained from time to time. It *should* take some work, some intentional effort, to forge through those early difficult stages. This stepdad's expectation for a quick family harmony has set him up for frustration and a critical attitude toward others.

Family stress is not an indication that you shouldn't have married in the first place. So roll up your sleeves, connect where you can, and stay the course—no matter how much work it takes.

> *Lord, when I get discouraged about family relationships, fill me with renewed strength and the unwavering conviction that the work will all be worth it someday.*

Occasionally Bow Out

ey stepparents, did you know you're the competition for your stepkids? Okay, that might be an overstatement, but sometimes it seems that way to kids. They feel as though they're competing with you for time and attention from their parent. And to be honest, on occasion they do need some focused time with their parent to bring stability in the midst of a whole lot of change.

So what can you do? You can give your spouse permission to spend one-on-one time with their kids; assure them that you're okay with that. (By the way, it'll be your spouse's job to maintain balance and spend time with you, too.) You can be involved in some family activities while bowing out of others, especially when noncustodial children come for the weekend and only have a little time to spend with their parent.

This approach diminishes the competition in the home and shows that you're a safe person. And when that happens, you're sure to come out a winner.

> *Give me the grace to encourage one-on-one time between my spouse and their biological children. Help my stepkids see me as a team member rather than their competition.*

Healthy Attitudes

Be honest—do you have an attitude problem? When it comes to co-parenting with an ex-spouse, adults need to adopt certain "co-parentudes." First and foremost, you need to always remember that you're on the same side. Divorce by nature is an adversarial process, but co-parenting needs to be a cooperative one. And to get there, you've got to remind yourself that you're on the same side—the side of your child. The interaction between your two homes should bless your child emotionally, behaviorally, and spiritually—not help you get your way. Put your child's needs above your own so you can co-parent peacefully.

And here's another attitude to adopt: Unless proven otherwise, presume the other home is competent to function without you. This means respecting their boundaries, giving up control, and letting them do things their way.

Hey, children aren't the only ones who need to watch their attitudes; sometimes adults need attitude adjustments, too.

Help me examine my attitudes, Lord. Show me which ones need to be dropped or reshaped for my family's well-being.

Find Something to Share

Let's say that you're new to being a stepparent or stepgrandparent and you're trying to figure out where to start. Bonding well with a stepchild really should be your first priority. And stepkids—of *every* age—are just like everyone else: They want to know how much you care before they care how much you know.

So be very intentional the first year of your blended family to invest in them. If you have some natural connecting points, be sure to make the most of those. For example, if you both like baseball, then make sure you play, watch, or talk about baseball. In addition, take interest in their interests. Notice what they enjoy and try to join in.

On the flip side, if they express an interest in your talents or skills, share what you are good at. Teach them how to play the guitar, to build something for the house, or to use a software program. Bottom line: Find things that make both of you smile—and share them.

God, please make me attentive to ways I can connect with my stepkids by enjoying common interests or learning something new from each other.

Be Like
the Highway Department

If you're a parent or stepparent, then you and the highway department have a lot in common. The freedom to drive does not mean you get to drive anywhere you want. The highway department determines that, along with a lot of other things. For instance, they pave a road where you're allowed to drive. Then they add a white line on the right side and a yellow on the left to assign your spot. Sometimes there's only one lane and sometimes there are multiple lanes. (That's when you do get to choose). They even determine how fast you're allowed to go.

So how is good parenting like being the highway department? Well, we set the boundaries for our kids, and we teach them where and how fast they can drive. But within that, we also give them lots of choices. And as we all know, the combination of freedom and boundaries—and a few tickets every now and then—makes for a well-trained driver.

Lord, give us the wisdom to set boundaries for our children that allow them just the right amount of freedom for making choices that help them learn valuable life lessons.

Through a Child's Eyes

Imagine your parents are madly in love. And then one day you see one of your parents kissing somebody else. How does that make you feel? Well, you probably feel a mixture of anger, confusion, disbelief, and fear. And questions—you have lots of questions swirling through your mind. Oh, and insecurity—you feel insecure because the foundation of your life is knowing where you came from, who loves you, and where home is.

So here's the deal: To a large degree, even if parents are divorced or one parent is deceased, a child—of any age—still feels all of this whenever they see a parent kissing someone else. It's just plain hard. Does this mean you should never kiss in front of them? No! Just don't overdo it until they appreciate your love for each other.

Parents, sometimes you need to see yourself through the eyes of your children, and then respond with compassion and thoughtfulness.

Heavenly Father, give us an understanding of how our children view our relationship. Show us ways we can increase their level of security and comfort when they need to accept a new person into their life.

Less Talk, More Action

Parents today use too many words. It's time we start talking less and acting more. We parents have the misguided idea that if we just talk long enough, our children will finally agree with us—and obey with joy and gladness in their hearts. Okay, sometimes that might actually happen. But for the most part it doesn't work out that way at all.

Naturally kids will want to know *why* they can't do something. And because teaching is an important part of parenting, you should give them an answer . . . once. After that, it's time to stop talking and do something.[25] "Samuel, I've already explained why you can't go. I'm walking away now, and if you keep badgering me about this, it will cost you . . . (and then name a developmentally appropriate consequence)." Then turn, walk away, and follow through on your promise. After a couple of times you'll make a true believer out of them.

So stop talking. And start doing.

Father, give me the wisdom to know when it's time to stop explaining, and the discipline to be consistent in following through with promised consequences.

Manage Yourself First

We all know that parenting is about managing your children, right? But consider this: Good parenting is often more about managing yourself than your kids. For example, Hector's daughter really pushed his buttons. She was direct, assertive, and questioned a lot of his decisions—all of which made him angry. In response, Hector often overreacted, even to the point of crushing her spirit.

Hector figured out that assertiveness threatened him, so people like his daughter—and his ex-wife—really pushed his buttons. Now, overreacting definitely hadn't worked out so well with his ex-wife. He finally understood that if he didn't want the same results with his daughter, he needed to take a good long look in the mirror and learn how to respond in a different way.

Yes, parenting is about strategies, but it is always first about managing ourselves. And hey, if you can't manage yourself, what makes you think you can manage your children?

Lord God, as I prayerfully examine my heart, please show me how I need to change the way I respond to family members.

Untie Your Child

When alternating between two homes, children just naturally get caught in loyalty binds sometimes, which is really unfortunate. Kids don't like having to choose between family members, but they often feel like they're being forced to. It's up to the adults to untie these binds and set the child free to adjust and grow within their new family dynamics.

Parents can give kids permission to enjoy themselves in the other home. For example, a mom might say, "Hey, have a great time with your stepmom this weekend." Words like this liberate a child's heart. Ex-spouses can act civilly toward one another and not criticize the other in front of the child. And church members can support the new marriage and welcome the blended family into their midst.

To untie loyalty binds for kids is to set them free to love. Now, that's something we all benefit from.

Lord, we never want our children to feel forced to take sides among family members. Help us speak words that will set them free to fully enjoy and love both their families.

Choose to Forgive

The Bible tells us to "Forgive as quickly and completely as the Master forgave you" (Colossians 3:13 THE MESSAGE paraphrase). The problem is that some people are just plain easier to forgive than others are. The ease with which we forgive someone is in part determined by the size and nature of the offense and by who committed it, right?

A lot of people consider their ex-boyfriend or girlfriend or ex-spouse an enemy. It's odd when you think about it: Romance makes you friends and a breakup makes you enemies. Jesus specifically told us to pray for our enemies. Even more than that, he instructed us to love them. And one great way to love them is to forgive them, just as the Lord has forgiven us.

Maybe you've been hurt so bad that it doesn't seem fair of God to expect you to forgive the other person. It might help to spend some time thinking about all that God has forgiven you. Then make this your prayer:

Lord, in response to your forgiving mercy, give me an overflowing cup of gratitude—so much so that it spills over onto those who have hurt me.

When Forgiveness Is Rejected

Have you ever had someone get mad at you—because you *forgave* them? I know, that really sounds strange, doesn't it? Forgiving someone pardons a debt and lets go of an offense. Normally that opens the door to reconciliation and restoration of the relationship. But what if the other person believes they didn't hurt you in the first place? In their eyes they don't owe you a thing. In that case, they might actually be offended that you forgave them. What are you supposed to do then?

Because reconciliation requires two people and forgiveness needs only one, you can still forgive the person in your heart. You can treat them as though they're forgiven—you just can't restore the relationship by yourself. Don't argue over whether forgiveness was necessary. Release your resentment for the offense and love them as best you can. Responding with a merciful heart just might soften their pride.

Father, give me the grace to offer forgiveness when I've been wronged, and the ability to keep loving the offender even if they never admit their wrongdoing.

Don't Take It Personally

Here's another tip for building a bridge to your stepchild's heart: Don't take rejection from them personally. "Yeah, right, Ron!" I can hear you saying. "That's easy to say, but so hard to do." Yes, it is hard—until we break it down and examine the motivation behind the behavior. I often find that when a child is struggling to accept you, it has more to do with their desire to stay in contact with their biological parent than it does with an actual rejection of you. Keeping that in mind is tough sometimes, but it helps to depersonalize their lack of acceptance.

Maybe it will help to remember this: Jesus was a good man and he always spoke the truth. But lots of people rejected him. Part of what kept him going was knowing his purpose and feeling the heavenly Father's approval—even when he didn't have it from the people around him. That sounds like a good model for stepparents to follow, too.

When I feel rejected by one of my stepchildren, Lord, remind me that you have appointed me to this role, and help me concentrate on fulfilling that purpose the best I can.

Difficult People, Part 1

Got any difficult people in your life? Yeah, me too. Wouldn't life be easier if everyone—from family and friends to co-workers and leaders—were nice people all the time? Then everyone could cooperate and get along. It would be great. But that just isn't real life, is it? If you're dealing with this issue right now, the first thing to remember is that you can't make unreasonable people become reasonable. You simply aren't that powerful. But what you *can* do is manage yourself. That's your strength.

One suggestion is to have flexible boundaries when you can. Also, go the extra mile sometimes. Go above and beyond what the other person deserves, and let your servant heart make a strong statement. A statement about integrity, humility, and not being self-centered. Who knows, maybe some of it will rub off on them. But even if it doesn't, you have testified through your actions to the grace of God in your life. And you can be sure that he has taken notice.

God, please give me a greater understanding of that difficult person in my life. Help me relax my expectations so that I can extend grace to them.

Difficult People, Part 2

Remember that advice I offered yesterday about dealing with difficult people? Well, sometimes you should just ignore it. Yes, sometimes going the extra mile is the best way to deal with unreasonable people. But at other times, the most loving thing you can do is to politely say no to their demands. Especially when going the extra mile contributes to a destructive pattern.

We all know there are some battles worth fighting. Whether it's saying no to a teen's repeated request to hang out with the wrong crowd, an ex-spouse's refusal to pay child support or spend time with their child, or a co-worker's habit of using harsh words, there comes a time to speak up for what's right.

Will our firmness change the difficult person? We can't know for sure. When smothered in grace and love, perhaps. But more important, it might change us.

Lord, help me know when it's time to take a stand and speak up about unhealthy habits or behavior. And give me ears to hear when someone feels they need to speak up to me.

Deal with Problems as They Arise

Some tips for a healthy marriage sound like no-brainers, like this one: Deal with problems as they arise. But for many of us, that's easier said than done. ("Hello, I'm Ron, and I'm a natural conflict avoider.") If you're like me and you prefer to avoid conflict rather than deal with it, you need to know something: That approach only guarantees that things will get much worse.

My research clearly shows that stepfamily couples who struggle in their relationship are much more likely to stockpile their issues until they result in escalating conflict, withdrawal, and emotional walls. Healthy couples, on the other hand, deal with problems as they arise, and they take seriously the process of solving problems together. That's a skill I had to learn. And boy, has it helped my marriage.

All couples have conflict. But it's best to periodically evaluate your relationship and ask yourself: Is the conflict managing you, or are you managing it?

Father, keep us willing to face each conflict as soon as it arises, learning problem-solving skills that allow us to work together as a team.

What Lies Beneath

Do you know how to listen *beneath* someone's words? Have you ever noticed that the masters of relationships know how to hear what's not being said—what lies beneath, if you will—and respond to *that* instead of the words on the surface? If you want to develop this skill, here's where to focus: Key in on the emotions that lie beneath the words. That's how you deepen the conversation and really connect with the other person.

With a co-worker who is griping about a manager, you might say, "It sounds like you're discouraged." With a child who is mad that you're not buying the shoes they wanted, ask what they're concerned about. You might discover they don't want to be made fun of. So maybe they're still not getting the shoes, but their concern of being isolated by kids at school—that's something you need to address.

Want to raise your relational IQ? Start listening to what lies beneath.

Help me train my ear to hear the true meaning of another person's words, and train my heart to respond in the appropriate way to their emotions, needs, and concerns.

When Parents Change the Rules

This one is written for your kids. Read and decide if you'll read it to them or have them read it themselves.

Hey kids, isn't it annoying when parents change the rules? Yeah, actually, it really is. You thought you knew what was expected of you and then, wham—suddenly you don't anymore. Now here's what's really annoying: They're allowed to do this. Being the parent gives them the prerogative to change the rules. And it happens all the time, doesn't it? They read a good book or go to a parenting class, and next thing you know, they change their expectations.

And then there are parent-stepparent changes. For years you could be sarcastic with your brothers, and then a stepparent enters the scene and they take it personally when you talk to your stepbrother that way. So now you're not allowed to be sarcastic. I know, it's a pain. And it would help if they didn't take things quite so personally. But let's face it—maybe you're just going to have to stop being sarcastic.

Lord, help me to respect the parental authorities placed over me. Help me to honor them with my cooperation and obedience.

August 20

A Bridge Finally Crossed

Looking back, Jessica sees that the bridge was always there. She wonders why it took her so long to finally cross it. Jessica and her stepfather started out on opposite sides of the ravine. "It took me years to appreciate what my stepfather did for me beginning at age thirteen," she said.

Now twenty-eight and a mother herself, Jessica finally gets it. "He provided for us and he loved me—even when I just couldn't let myself love him. I don't know why; I just couldn't. But eventually I relaxed and let him in, and now, we have an awesome relationship. What a blessing he has been in my life."

Like adoptive parents for a child without a home, stepparents can be God's provision for a child after divorce or the death of a parent. Finding love and acceptance may take a while, but when love builds a bridge, be sure to cross over to the other side. You'll probably look back and wonder why you waited so long.

Heavenly Father, help my love build a bridge to my child's heart that is irresistible and lets them know it's safe to cross over.

Be an Anchor

Grief is something we can all relate to, isn't it? Whenever we experience a loss of any kind, we need anchors to hold us steady in the midst of the storm. Those anchors can be psychological, relational, or spiritual in nature. For example, children need the consistent, comforting presence of the people they hold most dear. Someone to help them deal with the loss, the changes it keeps bringing, and what it means for their life over time. And they need perspective on how a good God could allow bad things to happen.

They also need permission to be happy one day and sad the next. And to repeatedly talk through their grief if they need to. In blended families, the wise stepparent will do all they can to make sure children and teens have all of these things. Because helping them grieve the past will lead them toward a happy, healthy future—and help them appreciate your role in that future.

> *Lord, help me live out my faith in such a way that my kids understand that you are the anchor that will hold through any storm in life.*

You Make a Difference

Know what happens when you choose to live like Jesus? You make a difference in somebody's life, whether you realize it or not. Being Christlike in our everyday lives leaves an indelible mark on those around us. Especially when our actions stand in direct contrast to other people's behavior.

Mandy had a mom and a stepmom as she grew up. Her mom spoke critically about her dad, always using a tone of frustration and bitterness. When Mandy's stepmom came into her life, she immediately noticed a difference. Her stepmom spoke to her dad with a sense of respect and warmth. Her devotion to him over the years made an intense impression on Mandy that shaped the type of woman, wife, and mother she wanted to be someday.

Today, Mandy is a loving wife because of her obedient stepmom's example. Does our behavior impact others? You bet it does.

Help me live each day with the awareness that someone is watching my habits and actions. May my example allow me to say along with Paul, "Be imitators of me, as I am of Christ" (1 Corinthians 11:1).

Living behind Enemy Lines

Can you imagine being caught behind enemy lines? In my book *The Smart Stepfamily*, I share that children who live between homes are like people who hold citizenship in two countries. They belong in each place, are relationally invested in the family of each home, and want peace between the two.

In response, one reader commented: "If parents only knew that, it would change their child's life. I am almost forty-four years old and my parents have been divorced for thirty-seven of them, yet I still feel as if I'm behind enemy lines when I visit or even speak about the other parent."

What a sad situation for all involved. So here's a message for parents, stepparents, and everyone in each country: It's up to you to forgive and to act as an ambassador of peaceful relations to the other country so that children—of every age—can feel safe at home.

Father, search my heart and convict me of any words, attitudes, or actions that make it seem like I consider my child's other home enemy territory. Help me contribute to peaceful relations between all family members.

Today you have a choice. If yours is a stepfather family read this page; if a stepmother family read the next page. Or if both of you are stepparents, you get a bonus dose of encouragement.

Stepdad: Knight in Shining Armor

This is going to sound a little strange, but stepdads, please don't try to be the knight in shining armor. Romance novels often characterize a man as a white knight who rides in and sweeps the woman off her feet and into wedded bliss. A lot of stepdads I know have also tried to be the knight who saves the day and fixes all the wrongs in the lives of his stepchildren.

I really appreciate that sentiment and the desire to help, but sometimes, that effort just backfires. So I have to say, "I know it sounds a little strange, but if you try to fix all the problems that other people created, your stepchildren may end up turning on you." Just come alongside the kids, embrace them, and try to be a steady, positive influence over time—not the white knight rushing in. So take off your armor and simply love them.

> *Father, give me realistic expectations for the role I can play in my stepkids' lives. While I can't wipe away all their past hurts, I commit to loving them the best I can.*

Stepmom:
A Challenging Role

You've heard of the "wicked stepmother," right? But what about the "plight of the stepmother"?

I'm quite certain that the average person doesn't have any idea just how challenging it is to be a stepmother. In nearly three decades of ministry I've yet to find a family role with more baffling expectations and dilemmas of responsibility than hers.

On one hand, she has all the responsibility of caring for her stepchildren, and her husband desperately wants her to have a mom-like relationship with them. But clearly, she is not their mom. Not emotionally, not psychologically, not relationally, not authoritatively—not even legally. Confusion and ambiguity surround her on every side. And yet everyone expects her to do her job well, including—or should I say, especially—herself.

No, this is not a "feel sorry for the stepmom" minute. This is a "cheer her on and lift her up" reminder. She has great responsibilities and many challenges. A little encouragement could go a long way.

Father, give me clarity as I fill my role of stepmom. I depend on your power to help me impact my chosen children for eternity.

Walk with Others

Would you like to grow in your relationship with the Lord? Do you want healthy family relationships? Then don't go it alone; walk with others. God said from day one that it wasn't good for man to be alone. We've always needed others in our lives.

At a recent stepfamily retreat I made sure the couples got a lot of time with other couples. They loved it! They talked, shared frustrations, and encouraged each other.

And even though they were from all over the country, I challenged them to stay connected with each another after the event ended. I urged them to go back to their local church and find other couples who could walk beside them along the blended family journey.

Want a healthy blended family? Don't go it alone. Get connected with other couples and study some good material . . . together.

> *Lord, I know you designed us to be part of a community. Please lead us to other families on this blended journey so we can share our lives as we learn and grow together, offering mutual support and encouragement.*

What Stepfamily Teaches about God

Have you ever noticed how God uses different stages of family life to teach us important spiritual lessons? For example, God uses the experience of childhood to teach us obedience and respect for authority. He uses becoming a parent to teach us how much he loves us. Singleness teaches us about the importance of friendships and brotherly love, marriage about sacrifice, and sex about surrender, vulnerability, and oneness.

Living in a blended family also holds valuable spiritual lessons for us. A second marriage helps some understand about mercy and second chances in life. And by extending grace to new family members, we see a reminder of God's grace. The kind of grace that always welcomes the outsider in and loves them unconditionally.

Healthy families—and stepfamilies—are one of God's most powerful tools for shaping us into the image of Christ. Why not take a few moments to consider what lessons your family is teaching you and your loved ones?

Lord Jesus, open our eyes to see how our family life is helping us grow to be more like you. We desire to learn all that you have to teach us.

Give the Very Best

What's your working definition of love? If you ask me, I think Hallmark had a pretty good definition. Well actually, it's an old ad campaign, but I think it captures the essence of what love does. Their well-known slogan was, "When you care enough to send the very best."

Let's try changing the word *send* to *give* and see how that works: When you care enough to *give* the very best. The best of what? Money, stuff, material possessions? How about the best of *yourself*? So in essence, love is "when you care enough about someone else to give them the best of you." Whether we're talking about a spouse, child, or other family member, I'd say that pretty well captures it.

When you think about it, that's what Jesus did for us—he gave the best of himself for us. And that's exactly what we should do for each other, every single day.

> *Jesus, help me follow your example of sacrificial love. Instead of giving my family the leftovers of my time and attention, I want to be my best and do my best for them.*

Blended Language

So, are you a *blended family* or a *stepfamily*? There's a whole lot of confusion about what term to use for the stepfamily. Ah, see there, I just used one option. Someone said, "But, Ron, we call our family a *blended family* because we're trying to blend everyone together." Yeah, that works. But then for some in the United States, a blended family means a biracial family that may or may not be a stepfamily.

There are others who call themselves a *merged family, remarried family, combined family,* or *instant family* (you mean like bad coffee?). Still others like the term *reconstituted family* (that just sounds like orange juice to me). Or, since there are two houses, what about *binuclear family*? Honestly, that makes me think, *"Stand back, she's going to blow!"*

Yes, there are a lot of labels to choose from these days. But no matter which one you prefer, just remember to act like a *family.*

> *Father, when we speak about our family, help us settle on labels that every member can feel comfortable using, always remembering that the operative word is* family.

Improve Your Communication Skills

I know a husband and wife who really get on each other's nerves. Whenever she wants more closeness or connection, she tosses hints in his direction and hopes he'll figure it out. And he—well, he just hears criticism instead of her intended request. So who do we blame? Their parents.

See, in her family, no one ever made a direct request for closeness because that would have felt too vulnerable. And in his family, indirect communication was how you let someone know they weren't pulling their weight—that they just weren't good enough. So you can blame their families of origin for their poor communication skills.

Now for the good news: I know a husband and wife who are learning to forgive, to be patient with each other's insecurities, and to speak more plainly about their needs. You can credit their Savior with that.

Show us how our communication styles hinder rather than nurture our relationship with each other and with our children. Teach us to speak in ways that help us understand each other better.

You Can't Hurry Love

Dear Ron,

My boyfriend and I just got engaged. How long will it take my kids and him to love each other?

Here's my reply to this woman's message:

Dear Eager Mom,

I have no idea. The amount of time it takes a stepparent and children to bond depends on a host of factors, a few of which are the child's age, what interests they share, the gender of the stepparent and child, and the child's relationship with the other biological parent. No one can predict this. What's most important, though, is that you don't let your eagerness rush the process. You want them—no, you need them—to love each other. If your need tries to orchestrate their relationship, it will probably backfire on you. So instead, be patient and prayerful. And give them enough space to figure one another out. They'll get there.

God, give me the wisdom, strength, and patience to allow new relationships to develop naturally, at their own pace. Help me resist the temptation to rush the process by learning to pray every time I feel the impulse.

Be Ready for Hot and Cold

A stepparent recently asked me, "Ron, what do I do with the hot and cold from my stepkids? One minute they love me, the next they want nothing to do with me." I've heard this sentiment expressed before. And that mixture of temperatures is one of the most confusing aspects of being a stepparent. One minute they like you, but then they feel weird about it, or disloyal to their parent, or confused about their emotions. So they back away.

How can you possibly thrive in the midst of this? First, have some compassion for how hard this is for the child. They aren't trying to be manipulative. They feel confused about your relationship just like you do. So give them some grace. Cut them a break. And second, enjoy when they are leaning toward you, but don't take it personally if they back up. Exercise your patience and give them all the time they need. Eventually, you'll notice that they're leaning away less and less.

Lord, help me always notice and make the most of those leaning-in moments, and give me patience during the times my stepkids back away from me.

Wait on God

Have you ever gotten tired of waiting on God? I know I have. Sarah got tired of waiting on God, too. The Bible tells us that she got tired of waiting for the child God had promised to her and her husband, Abraham. So she took measures into her own hands.

Sarah gave her maidservant to her husband, thinking they could have the promised child through her (see Genesis 16). But all Sarah did was create one of the first recorded stepfamilies along with a whole lot of competition, jealousy, and resentment within her home.

You know, becoming impatient with God and taking control to meet your selfish desires is *never* a good idea. And it almost always causes trouble for us and for those closest to us. As for me, I hate waiting. But trusting God's timing means that he's in control and I'm his servant. And that's always a good thing for both me and my family.

> *Father, I trust you enough to wait for your timing, even when that's really hard to do. If I start to think of ways that I can work things out myself, please stop me.*

Talk Your Way In

Are you playing the game of Lock Out? When I was a kid, we played a simple game I call Lock Out. A group of us would lock arms and make a circle; someone on the outside would try to break into the circle. The harder the outsider pushed, the more the circle banded together to keep them out.

Sometimes stepfamilies play this game, too. An outsider stepparent or stepsibling is trying to break into the circle of insiders and find acceptance. Some insiders keep them out on purpose, perhaps because of jealousy, insecurity, or a refusal to accept the new family dynamics. Others do so inadvertently due to a lack of sensitivity or understanding.

Now, here's the secret to getting inside: Don't push. When you do that, the members of the circle just tighten their grip and close ranks. Instead, walk up next to them and stand there. Talk, interact, and get to know them. Eventually they'll unlink their arms and let you in.

Lord, help me remember that relationships cannot be forced. Make me the kind of spouse and parent that my family members want to invite into their circle.

The Stepparenting Roller Coaster

Parenting in a complex family is like . . . riding a roller coaster.

Before I explain, let me confess that sometimes, to teach a principle, we family educators are guilty of oversimplifying things. For example, I've often said to stepparents, foster parents, and grandparents raising kids that there are stages to parenting; your developing role with a child might progress from babysitter, to an uncle or aunt, to being a bonus parent.

But bonding is not linear. In reality, it's more like up and down, in and out, round and round, one step forward and two steps back. And just when you think you're getting somewhere, the roller coaster turns you upside down. I know—it's really confusing, isn't it? But believe it or not, you're actually getting somewhere. The point is that thinking in terms of stages gives you an idea of what might be ahead, but real life is more complex than that. And, yes, roller coasters can make you nauseous, but they do have their rewards, too.

Loving Father, help me stay close to you so that I can remain steady through all the ups and downs of parenting in a blended family.

Be Trustworthy

Trust calms the heart. Which is why we all need to be trustworthy. Without trust relationships begin to fall apart. Whether we're talking about trusting our politicians, our parents, a salesman, a spouse, or God, trust is a vital ingredient in any relationship. So we need to ask ourselves: How can *I* be trustworthy?

Family therapist Terry Hargrave says that trustworthy relationships include a strong balance of giving and receiving love. Trustworthy people are predictable—meaning they're responsible and reliable about keeping their promises. They're also open and they allow other people to see them as they really are. They're not afraid to be vulnerable.

Now, God is all of these things—and aren't you glad he is! If we want to be like him . . . and want strong, intimate relationships where people feel safe and loved, then we need to be trustworthy people. Are you a trustworthy spouse? Parent or stepparent? If not, then you can't expect your home to feel emotionally safe and loving.

Lord, help me examine my character and behavior to pinpoint areas where I can improve my level of trustworthiness.

Family Pictures, Part 1

He wants me to throw away all our old family photos."

My response to this statement is always the same: "No, don't do it." Trying to erase someone's past because you're uncomfortable with it simply does not work.

I cringe whenever I hear about a stepparent who asks their spouse to get rid of old family photos or who redecorates the entire house soon after moving in. The message is "Your past is gone and I don't want you to have any attachment to it—whether good, bad, or ugly." Well, that "out with the old, in with the new" approach is pretty offensive, especially to stepkids. And if you weren't insecure about your place in their lives before, you really should be now.

Listen, it's much better to embrace their past than try to erase it. Step in with grace. That's what they'll judge you on.

Father, I promise to accept my spouse's and stepkids' pasts as part of their identity. Now help me devote myself to making their future something to treasure.

Family Pictures, Part 2

If there's a picture in your home and you're not in it, I have a suggestion: Say to one of your children, "Tell me about that." Yesterday I encouraged stepparents not to get rid of pictures of their spouse's prior family. Well, today I want to take that a step further: Ask the kids to tell you about those pictures.

You know, pictures and videos from the past represent how life was and usually capture the best of times. Only a foolish stepparent would try to erase or ignore that history; doing so implies that the kids themselves are a mistake. The wise stepparent will encourage the kids to tell the stories behind the pictures.

Honoring and celebrating your stepchild's previous family story celebrates them—their worth, their value, talents, and heritage. Look at it from their perspective. When you embrace their past, you embrace them. And that makes it more likely that they'll want to embrace you back.

Never let me miss an opportunity to encourage my stepchildren to talk about their special memories, even the ones that don't include me.

Family Pictures, Part 3

To kids, a picture of a parent not living with them is worth a lot more than a thousand words. You know, talking about prior family pictures in a stepfamily tends to bring out people's passions. Biological parents want to preserve pictures for their children, and rightly so. Kids need pictures and videos of family members who live in other homes. And sometimes stepparents want to know if there are appropriate boundaries for where such pictures are displayed.

Well, yes, there are. Think public and private. As long as it's not intended to be disrespectful, kids should be free to keep or display important pictures and videos in their private space. Their bedroom and mobile devices are good examples of appropriate locations. But if a child has the idea to hang a life-size wedding portrait of their biological parents over the mantle in the living room? In that case you can definitely say no.

Father, keep me free from petty jealousies toward my stepchild's biological parents. At the same time, help us grow so close that they can't picture a life without our relationship in it.

Use the Right Blueprint

Have you ever tried to build a home—without a blueprint? You don't really have to answer that one. We all know what a big mistake that would be. But just as bad, some couples start to build their stepfamily home with someone else's blueprint. Of course, they often don't realize they're doing that. But if you take the biological family blueprint and try to build a blended family home, it will weaken the home.

For example, the role of a stepparent is very different from that of a biological parent. So if you use the wrong blueprint, everything falls down. But blended family blueprints make sense of this. And they take into consideration how loss affects kids, the stress during holidays, the potential conflicts between homes. . . . The list goes on and on.

Yes, stepfamilies need blueprints designed for stepfamilies. Get your hands on those, and the foundation, the walls, and the roof of your home will be rock solid.

Lord, lead us to the resources that can help us build our family with the right blueprint. Most of all, we pray that our foundation will be based on the Rock, Jesus Christ.

Dysfunctional Families

Have you ever thought about how dysfunctional the families of the Bible were? Yes, God's plan for the family is ideal, but none of his followers were perfect. There's Abraham, who lied on two occasions, denying that Sarah was his wife. Rebecca played favorites with her children and helped one deceive her husband, Isaac. Jacob had four wives but only deeply desired one of them. He favored Joseph so much that his ten older half-brothers hated him, sold him into slavery to get rid of him, and then lied to their father about it.

David also had multiple wives, and his family story included a premeditated murder to cover up an affair, an out-of-wedlock pregnancy, and a son who raped his half-sister only to have a half-brother hunt him down in revenge and kill him. Talk about dysfunctional!

What can we learn from these messed-up families? Here's the most obvious lesson: You can be far less than perfect and still be redeemed and used by God for his purposes. Thank you, God!

Thank you, Father, for your mercy and grace that can redeem even the most imperfect people and dysfunctional families and bring beauty out of our messes.

Walk a Mile

All right, parents, here's a challenge for you: Walk a mile in your kids' shoes. As a dad, every once in a while I challenge myself to walk a mile in my kids' shoes. *What's it like to be them at this season of their life?* I wonder. Asking that question periodically helps me be more in tune with what they need from me. What's it like to be with their friends or go to their school? How is it living in my home with our financial situation, parenting style, and stressors?

Parents in stepfamilies have other questions to ask as well: What's it like to go between homes with different rules and expectations? To grieve a deceased parent or family fractured by divorce? To receive criticism from a stepparent, or feel guilty for liking a stepparent? And what's it like to talk to God about all of this?

Let me encourage you to take time *today* to walk a mile in their shoes.

Give me greater understanding of what my children experience from day to day. Show me how I can support them in their walk of faith.

Finding New Hope

Tragedy and hope make a strange combination, don't they? Sheri Ladley lost her husband, James, in New York City on September 11, 2001. Her two children lost their father. Their family lost balance, stability, and joy. There's no question that the 9/11 attacks were tragic for all Americans. But for Sheri and her kids, and for James' extended family, it was deeply tragic, a personal loss that's hard to fathom.

Since that day our country has rebuilt some of what it lost. Sheri's family has, too. She remarried a few years later and had a daughter whose middle name is Hope. Although the painful memories will never completely fade, Sheri and her children have learned to embrace happiness and joy once again.

Take a minute today to pause and remember the people we lost and the national tragedy that changed everything for so many of us. And let's cling tightly to hope—and to the One who heals, restores, and makes all things new.

Loving Father, on this anniversary of such a tragic event, we ask you to turn our hearts to you as the source of our strength and hope for the future.

Waiting for Reconciliation

In Romans 12:18 Paul tells us, "If possible, so far as it depends on you, live peaceably with all." Well, that's just fine when circumstances allow for it, but when a friend or family member walks away or refuses your attempts to have a relationship it's not up to you. So what are you supposed to do then?

I think there's a delicate balance between chasing after someone you love because you want them to know you care, and giving them space to turn around and see you. Often, hounding them only serves to push them farther away.

I've worked with a lot of parents who are heartbroken because one of their kids won't come for visitation. Whatever the reason, they just refuse to engage. No matter how frustrated, the parent needs to stay determined to reconcile—and close enough to be found when the child turns around. And because waiting is hard, lots of prayer will be needed.

Help me do all I can to bring reconciliation and peace to broken relationships. And make me willing to wait as long as it takes for someone's heart to change.

Event Etiquette

Does your child live in two different homes? If so, you might want to consider following some guidelines for event etiquette when attending their activities. We know that kids love it when their parents attend their recitals, concerts, sporting events, and school productions. But their enthusiasm dissolves if co-parents make it stressful. To make any event affirming for your child, be sure to mind your etiquette:

- Sit where you feel comfortable and be respectful to the other parent as you walk in and out.
- After the event, let your child hug or talk to each parent no matter who currently has visitation privileges.
- To keep the event safe for everyone, don't discuss parenting matters at the event. That turns a recital into a business conversation and takes the focus off your child. You can talk about that later. Let this moment simply be about celebrating your child.

Father, during our children's activities and events, remind us to drop our personal agendas and focus on making good memories that build up and encourage our kids.

Look through the Window

Did you know that sometimes anger is a window into a child's grief? For kids, sometimes "mad" is really "sad." Young children, for example, may not have adequate words to express their pain or loss, so they use their actions instead. Disruptive behavior could really just be internalized tears. In teenagers, an uncooperative attitude or an angry defiance could also point to the grief they feel over family circumstances they dislike but can't change.

Parents, grandparents, and family friends should learn to look beyond the child's behavior and address the heart of the issue. You could open a conversation by saying something like, "I know you're really upset right now. I'm wondering if you're sad about something, too?" You might not be able to fix the circumstances of their life, but listening to their words and hugging their heart will let them know they aren't alone.

Give me discernment to see past my child's negative behavior and attitudes so I can understand the real issues they need help with. And even when they feel unable to talk with an adult or friend, teach them to pour out their heart to you.

Move in with Tact

Here's a message especially for stepdads: "Slow down. Have some tact, okay?"

We guys are just natural fixers, aren't we? Some of us get paid to do that all day long. But all of us feel pretty good about ourselves when we've conquered a problem.

Unfortunately, that makes it easy for us to miss an important fact: Fixing requires tact and timing.

Imagine a new stepdad who is trying to be accepted and find his place in the home. If he comes in like a bull in a china shop, whew—something fragile is bound to get broken. And that's just the problem: Your position in the family is fragile at this point.

So don't try to force your way in, right every wrong, or conquer every mountain without first consulting your wife about her kids. Be prepared to lower your expectations for a quick resolution. Move in with tact, respect, patience, and lots of prayer. That's how things get done on the construction site of a blended family.

Lord, temper my desire to fix problems with the wisdom to handle situations with tact, sensitive timing, and lots of prayer.

September 16

National Stepfamily Day

D id you know that today is National Stepfamily Day? Started in 1997, National Stepfamily Day is now recognized by all fifty states, along with Canada and the United Kingdom. Given that half of all Americans are now or will be part of a blended family, it shouldn't surprise us that there's actually a day to celebrate being in a stepfamily. Even those who aren't part of a blended family likely know someone who is among their circle of friends, co-workers, or neighbors.

And just what are we celebrating? According to the official proclamation, "National Stepfamily Day is a day to celebrate the many invaluable contributions stepfamilies have made to enriching the lives and life experience of the children and parents of America and to strengthening the fabric of American families and society."

All I can say is "Amen to that!"

Take some time today to lift up stepfamilies around the nation, including those of government leaders, first responders, military personnel, and pastors. Pray for children who have lost a parent to death and for those living in two homes between divorced parents, and for extended stepfamily members, that they, too, may find their place and feel at home.

I Destroyed His Dreams

Today's thought may be a little tough to read. It shares a reality for many children (although not all) with the hopes that it will give you some much-needed perspective.

"You see, Ron, I think I destroyed his dreams."

This stepdad shared an insight with me that unfortunately took him many years to recognize. But when it finally dawned on him, it hit him like a ton of bricks. He said, "When I married my stepson's mother, I destroyed his dream of his parents ever getting back together."

Sounds sad, but it's often true. Many kids of divorce do hold on tightly to that dream. So it's really hard when a parent's remarriage makes it impossible for their most cherished hope to come true. And that explains why the boy wasn't so welcoming to the stepdad. For a long time. The stepdad's realization helped soften his heart toward the boy, and in time they found their way to each other.

Dreams do die hard. And after that, sometimes new dreams begin.

Give me understanding to recognize how each member of my family struggles with broken or lost dreams. Help us make room for new ones together.

Honeymoon at the End of the Journey

Sometimes the road to marital happiness is a lot longer than you thought it would be. For newlyweds, dreams of marital happiness often quickly crash into reality, often before the honeymoon is over. Nearly every couple experiences some discouragement on their way to happily ever after.

In stepfamily couples, the premarriage fantasy of marital peace and harmony usually doesn't become reality for five or more years because it takes the family about that long to figure out how to be a family. Merging different individuals and different cultures takes a while to accomplish successfully. That's why I like to joke that for stepcouples, the honeymoon comes at the end of the journey, not at the beginning.

Yes, the road to the honeymoon—or maybe I should say the "family-moon"—may be a lot longer than you thought. But once you arrive, boy, is it worth the journey!

Help us set aside our unrealistic expectations about marital and family bliss as we go through the necessary process of blending together. However long or difficult the journey, we trust that the end result will be worth it.

No Pain, No Gain

S orry, Ron, this might hurt for your own good."

I'm lying in the dental chair getting my teeth cleaned—which is uncomfortable to begin with—and the hygienist, who is pushing on a crown, says, "Sorry I'm having to be so assertive." I mumble back, "It's okay; I'm not feeling any pain." To which she says, "Then I'm not doing my job."

In many areas of life, pain means growth, doesn't it? For example, when was the last time you read God's Word and let it step on your toes? Or made yourself attend a parenting or marriage or relationship conference? Or walked into a church even though you knew you wouldn't know anyone there? Or took a risk and made a sacrifice for a family member who is closed toward you?

Our natural instinct is to avoid any source of pain. But pain can indicate that something is being healed, repaired, or strengthened. (Just ask any athlete or doctor.) Sometimes no pain equals no gain.

Lord, make me willing to embrace what is uncomfortable, convicting, or even downright painful if it means healthy growth for me or for my family.

Waiting for Rewards

Parenting over the long haul is tough. And stepparenting is *really* tough. But let me back up a bit. Not all stepparents feel like their job is tough. But clearly, on the whole, if you just sit and listen to stepparents for a while you'll see that when it comes to discipline, finding acceptance, dealing with the other home—even coping with the negative stereotypes of society—stepparents have many challenges. And they also have fewer rewards.

Of course, biological parents have challenges, too. But on a regular basis they also enjoy sweet exchanges with their kids—a handmade card or drawing, a sincere thank-you, or a teachable moment that draws parent and child together. Stepparents enjoy these kinds of moments, too, but with much less frequency—and with less certainty. And that's why stepparents need a *really* big hug.

Father, thank you for placing me in this role of stepparent. On days when it feels like a thankless task, remind me that my rewards for a job well done ultimately come from you.

Be Flexible

Are you constantly coming up against barriers in your marriage? Here's a simple but powerful tip: Adapt to life as needed.

I'm sure we can all agree that life has a way of throwing us curves. And when it does, flexible people find a way to adapt. They either get creative in handling their differences or they figure out how to compromise in order to work through a disagreement. But it's more than that—these husbands and wives are willing to change *themselves* if necessary to grow together through a circumstance.

For other couples, attitudes of rigidity and stubbornness keep them stuck in a rut. They simply aren't willing to change. And they refuse to consider the other's point of view. So they just keep beating their heads against the same wall expecting it to move.

Do you want a healthy blended marriage? Then trust God with what you can't control and be willing to adapt to those circumstances . . . together.

> *Lord God, whenever we face tough situations, help us be flexible enough to adapt or compromise as needed, always trusting in you and in each other.*

Stop the Argument Insanity

B elieve it or not, today I'm going to reveal the secret of how to get your child to stop arguing with you. Did you realize that arguing is an act of cooperation? If that sounds strange, think about it this way: A parent who can't get their child to stop arguing is a parent who is arguing with their child. Come on! Be the parent. Stop entertaining the argument—first, by standing there and listening to it, and second, by fueling it with a reply.

Yes, kids need to know the reason for your rule or decision. After all, our goal is to move our children toward the values behind those rules, not just force them into mindless obedience. But once an adequate explanation has been given, stop standing there and empowering them to argue with you.

Just turn and walk away. And then pick up the clothes they refused to wash themselves and put those clothes in time-out . . . for two weeks.

Father, help me get rid of communication habits that encourage or perpetuate arguing within our family.

Pick Your Battles

R on, as the biological dad I agree that I should make my wife—my kids' stepmom—a high priority in the home. But does that mean I *always* have to agree with her?"

No, it doesn't. Finding unity as a parenting team is certainly important, especially when it comes to setting boundaries and standards for the home. But there are some negotiations every family faces that don't necessarily represent mountains to die on.

For example, when it comes to day-to-day preferences regarding family activities or which television shows to watch, one parent sometimes agrees with the kids rather than their spouse. And that's perfectly fine. What you *don't* want is a repetitive pattern of disagreement between the parents concerning significant family matters. And if you find yourself repeatedly falling into that hole, climb out fast. Or else the jealousy and insecurity will just get worse.

> *Father, help us recognize which decisions are okay to be divided on and which issues call for agreement between my spouse and me. Help our family hold on to a spirit of unity even during times of disagreement and negotiation.*

Ride Out the Storm Together

My wife once asked me: "What happened to our teenage son? He used to be sweet. Now he's just a pain." Can you relate to that sentiment? Parent educator Roger Allen said that all kids are subject to a relapse of the terrible twos—usually around age fifteen. It's not pleasant but it really is predictable: Your loving, huggable child who used to adore you suddenly becomes sarcastic and prickly.

Adolescence naturally shakes up any home. The teen is wrestling with their emerging identity, changes in their body, and the awkward challenges of their social group.

Blended families can be shaken by this, too. What once seemed like smooth sailing for the family can quickly become rough waters when kids turn irritable. If this describes your situation right now, pull back and regroup as parents so you can ride out the storm united. And remember that like the terrible twos, this too will pass.

Lord, during difficult transitions in our children's lives, show us how to support them and help them through to the other side.

When the Child's Other Home Is Not Faithful

We expect the world to try to pull our kids away from Christ, but sometimes it's their own family that moves them in the wrong direction. For millions of kids of divorce, the beliefs taught in their two homes couldn't be farther apart. One mom asked how she could share the gospel with her two girls who live with their unbelieving father. Of course she's praying for them, but she worries that the other home's influence will squash their trust in the Lord.

In addition to living by example, this mom can also share biblical wisdom and insight. Even when distance separates her from her girls, she can use texting or social media to nurture their faith. And whenever the kids visit, she can share her faith community with them.

One word of warning: If you want to help your child's faith grow, don't shove the Bible down their throat. Teach it and live it out; let them see the Good News come alive in you.

Guide us as we share your truth with our children every chance we get. Please protect them from influences that push them toward ungodly thinking or behavior.

No Fear in Marriage

Every marriage is susceptible to fear and insecurity. But I believe, on average, that stepfamily marriages are even more vulnerable to the fear of a breakup, especially when one or both of you have experienced that before. Pray, then, specifically for the Lord's help to combat the fear that builds walls and fosters self-protection instead of sacrifice.

Fear is a big issue for humans. I know this because nearly 150 times Scripture tells us not to worry about life or be afraid. God often reassured his people when they were facing the unknown; he understood they would be apprehensive. He said, "Do not be afraid" or "Fear not" to many heroes of the faith like Abraham, Isaac, Jacob, Moses (three times), the Israelites (twelve times), Joshua (three times), Gideon, Elijah, Jeremiah (twice), Mary and Joseph, Peter, the disciples (ten times), and Paul (twice).

Listen, fear of the unknown or being hurt again in a relationship is understandable. But what should you do? Set aside fear and trust him.

Lord, replace any fear in our marriage with confidence, and worry with security. And give us dedicated hearts—to love, serve, and cherish as long as we both shall live.

Through Heaven's Eyes

What do you see when you look at yourself through heaven's eyes? The Bible reveals what you *ought* to see: someone who is deeply loved, forgiven, and cherished. The words of Titus 3 tell us that God saved us by his mercy, so that by his grace we might become his heirs (see Titus 3:4–7). Did you catch that? Despite our sinfulness, we have been reborn and made new in Jesus Christ. Now we are heirs of the King.

If Jesus is your Savior, you have a brand-new identity as God's child and heir. You are a person of surpassing value with a worth that doesn't have to be earned by your own efforts. What's even better, your worth can never be diminished or taken away by anyone or anything.

Now share that worth with the person next to you, especially the person you get along with least well, so they too can see their value reflected through heaven's eyes.

Father, empower me to live in a way that's worthy of my new identity as your child and heir. Show me how to help others discover their worth in your eyes.

September 28

The Ties That Bind

The French poet Jean Baptiste Legouve once said, "A brother is a friend given by Nature." Well, what if the brother was given not by nature, but by marriage? Millions of Americans have a half-sibling or a stepsibling. And just as with full siblings, the ties that bind vary from close to distant and everything in between. But there are some things parents and stepparents can do to help foster stronger bonds between half- and stepsiblings.

Initially, help kids come together around common interests. Time spent playing a game, having a conversation, or attending and cheering for one another's extracurricular activities make for a good beginning. Next, orchestrate experiences where they get to build memories together and figure out who one another are. Service or mission projects are wonderful opportunities for this, as is helping a neighbor.

Of course, you can't orchestrate everything. Eventually, they'll have to figure out their relationship for themselves and take it from there. But in the meantime, you can encourage them to love each other by loving them.

Lord, help us love and parent each of our children in ways that encourage them to develop close friendships with each other that will last a lifetime.

Step-Money: #1 Cause of Divorce?

I'm sure you've heard that money problems are the number one cause of divorce, right? Actually that's not accurate. Yes, it's true that the top issues couples argue about are money, sex, and parenting. But the reason they can't resolve those arguments is because of how they argue, their personal agendas, their conflicting values about money, their selfishness—and their stubbornness. Those things are what turn a topic like money into a source of contention.

So what's the solution? The first step is making sure that your values about money line up with God's values. That's what will unify a couple and give them a compass to go by.

Only then can you address the actual logistics of money management. And for stepcouples, it can get especially complicated with all the different assets, debts, dynamics, and people to consider. For those reasons, getting specific guidance and advice for your family circumstances can be well worth the cost.

Father, we ask you to show us areas where our financial values contradict your values and your will. Help us use our financial resources in ways that honor you.

Learn to Lose Yourself

What do you do when family relationships compete? Usually we think of family members as standing up for each other, but sometimes we're against one another. For example, siblings can become rivals for their parents' attention or favor. This is something that happened repeatedly in the families of the Bible, like when Joseph's half-brothers despised him for being the favored child (see Genesis 37).

In stepfamilies there's a natural temptation to compete for the time and energy of others. Stepchildren want time with their biological parent who is now shared with the stepparent. Children who live with Mom want lots of exclusive time with Dad when they go to his house for the weekend.

The secret to navigating this competition is for each of you to let go of selfishness and consider the needs of others above your own. And in doing that, you'll discover one of the paradoxes of living God's way: There's just something about losing yourself that helps you find yourself.

Lord God, we ask your help in protecting our family from an unhealthy spirit of rivalry and competition. Teach us how to lose ourselves in serving each other.

Spiritual Intimacy

Husbands and wives share many things, but does your marriage reflect what it means to share the Lord? Lots of couples enjoy watching movies together, reading books and then discussing them, or any number of activities and hobbies. But ask them how they "share the Lord together" and they freeze up. Yet spiritual intimacy is vital to any healthy marriage. Thankfully, any couple can foster it.

You might start out by sharing a thought about God and then letting the other respond. Or read one Scripture together and talk about what it means or how you might apply it. It doesn't have to be a whole chapter, just one verse or passage. Speaking of verses, you could talk about the words of a hymn or worship song and what they teach you about Christ. And occasionally, serve beside one another. It could be an organized service project or just raking a neighbor's leaves. The point is to minister together and talk about it.

Whenever you share the Lord, you deepen your marriage.

Father, help us learn to become comfortable in sharing our personal faith with each other as we study your Word and serve together.

October 2

Don't Assume—
Just Listen!

When it comes to listening, most of us assume that we're pretty good listeners. Now here's the irony of that statement: We assume we're good listeners, but making assumptions actually makes us bad listeners. I did this to my wife *again* the other day. She was telling me her opinion about a parenting matter and I felt sure I knew where she was headed, so I jumped right in. Except I was wrong about my assumptions, so my interruption only served to frustrate my wife and sidetrack our conversation.

Whether it's a child or friend or family member, we all make assumptions that can short-circuit communication. So what can we do to improve our listening skills? First, be humble enough to admit that you can't read minds—or hearts. And then, remind yourself to be "quick to hear" and "slow to speak" as James 1:19 advises. Check your assumptions at the door so that you'll be free to fully listen and understand.

God, when I'm in a conversation, help me set aside my assumptions and give the other person my full attention to hear what they are truly communicating.

Your Flexibility Muscle

So, how strong is your flexibility muscle? Just like the human body, families need a good combination of flexibility and stability to stay healthy over time. Your flexibility muscle allows you to maintain balance. A pair of Olympic ice skaters need adequate strength and stability when leaning on each other. But they also need enough flexibility to bend, spin, or move in sequenced motion.

In a similar way, parents should have consistent expectations for children, but be prepared to adjust those expectations as the kids grow and mature. Couples need clear values for spending money so they can manage the family budget over time, but they still need to be flexible when life demands a shift in financial priorities. And given all the changes stepfamilies naturally have to face, blended families need parents to be strong leaders who know when to bend and when not to.

Lord, show us when we need to be flexible in order to best meet our family's needs while preserving a foundation of stability and strength.

Managing Conflict, Part 1

Every couple has conflict. But having the right tools in your toolbox will help you manage it. There are lots of little things that healthy couples do to manage conflict in their marriage. Here are a couple of suggestions:

- Make a deliberate effort to deal with your anger. Literally bite your tongue if you have to. Back off until you calm down. Process what is making you angry and get ahold of yourself. Then (and only then) you can share your concern with your spouse.
- Don't be an archeologist—somebody who digs up the past and sheds a light on it. I don't think you want to play that role in your marriage. Bringing up old hurts or comparing your spouse to their parents just complicates the current issue. Instead, focus on the here and now.

Make resolving the conflict your goal. Because whenever you fight to win, your marriage loses out.

Heavenly Father, help us learn to handle conflict in ways that strengthen our relationship instead of weakening it.

Managing Conflict, Part 2

very conflict has its own little dance routine; partners often fall into two categories. Which one are you: a "Distancer" or a "Pursuer"? Sometimes we do a combination of both, but everyone tends to gravitate toward one or the other. In marriage, for example, Distancers try to ease a tense situation by withdrawing or minimizing the conflict. But Pursuers chase discussion about the problem; they try to help by getting the issue resolved and out of the way.

Notice that both dancers are trying to help. But if you're a Pursuer, it sure is annoying in the heat of battle when the Distancer starts shutting down. And Distancers really don't like how determined Pursuers are to keep the discussion going. So how in the world do you resolve this impasse? Instead of repeating your usual steps, each of you has to learn how to stand still and pay attention. When each partner learns to better manage themselves, then the two of you can gracefully dance right through the conflict.

Lord, show me the steps I need to take in order to help resolve disagreements and conflicts in a healthy way.

Help Them Learn to Share

Learning to share a parent is really hard for children. Even if you've never been in that situation, maybe you've had a close friend that you trusted deeply and then you had to share them with someone else. Remember how that felt?

When a parent dies or when parents divorce, children experience many losses. Holding tightly to a parent is one way they find security in the midst of the storm. But when new stepfamily members enter the picture, the child is forced to share a parent who represents their source of safety and security. And to them, it feels like another loss.

Don't be surprised by the mixed reactions this commonly brings out in children. Instead, engage the child with openness and encourage them to talk about how it makes them feel. While you're listening, be sure to say something like "I care and you're not alone," which ultimately is exactly what they need to know.

Father, help us encourage our children to talk about their sense of loss so we can show them how much they have gained.

Part-Time Kids

Hey, Ron, how can a parent balance their expectations for part-time kids?"

Some single-parent and blended families know how tough it is to balance your expectations for kids you have only on the weekends or during the summer. The situation is especially tricky when you have other children full-time.

Personally, I think you should try to spend some focused time with children who come on the weekends. Even if it means disappointing other family members, try to carve out some one-on-one time to make the most of your limited opportunities. But also make time for all of the kids to be together. And be careful to never show preference in gift giving or demonstrating affection.

As for chores, you just can't expect a two-days-a-week child to carry the load of a seven-days-a-week child. Still, nobody gets a free pass. On the days they're in your home, everyone should pull their own weight.

Father, help us always be mindful to let each one of our children know they are equally valued and loved regardless of how much time they spend at our home.

Expectation vs. Reality

It turns out there's a big difference between expectation and reality. For example, the expectation is that having a baby is one of the greatest moments of your life (which of course it is), but the reality is that childbirth hurts—a lot! (So I've heard.)

The expectation is that going to college is an achievement to be proud of, but the reality is that getting that degree takes a great amount of time, effort, and money. Saving for retirement is wise, but the discipline to save is challenging. Starting a blended family is exhilarating, but making it work is often harder than expected.

Honestly, this shouldn't surprise us. We all know that anything worth having takes work and commitment. Most great expectations present struggles of some kind. You'd think we would get used to it and trust God to see us through to the reality. Because once we do learn to trust him implicitly, we have every reason to expect great things.

God, I accept that a healthy, close-knit family takes a lot of time and work. And I trust you to help us make that a reality as we follow your leading.

Teaching Respect

Tasha contacted us on social media. She was desperately trying to help her husband, her children's stepfather, to be respected by her children—and we wanted to help out.

Early in a stepfamily, stepparents walk a tightrope. They're trying to build a relationship with the kids, establish their role in the home, and contribute to the parenting all at the same time.

When it comes to the kids, the tightrope has to do with respect. When Tasha's husband would ask her kids to do something, they would go ask their mom if they had to follow through. Obviously, they viewed her as the authority and not him.

I reassured Tasha that this is a common dynamic in newly blended families. Her role is naturally clear to them, but his is not. So what she needed to do was to back him up and to communicate the message that respecting her meant also respecting him.

> *Help us make it clear to our children that just as we respect each other as partners, we expect them to recognize that both of us have authority over them.*

Pray Over
What You Can't Control

Because we parents love our kids, we stay vigilant to protect them from harm. So it's really sobering when we think about all the things that we can't control. We can't control what another kid says to them at school or how a teen drives when giving them a ride. No matter how hard we try, we can't completely control all the negative influences they encounter online or the germs they're exposed to at school and other public places. *I know, I know—I'm making you a little anxious right now.*

Stepparents also have things they can't control: What a parent in the other home says about them. How quickly a stepchild will open their heart to them. And they can't change the fact that they'll never be their spouse's first love. *Okay, now you're really anxious.*

So what can parents do? We can pray. And we can cast our anxieties on the One who can be trusted with all the things we can't control.

Father, show me how to release all my concerns and worries into your loving, all-powerful hands. I choose your peace over my desire to control everything that affects my family.

Pray for Open Hearts

Billy Graham described prayer as a two-way conversation between you and God.

I strongly encourage you to engage in that conversation on a daily basis, always making sure to pray for your family. Here's one thought you might add to the conversation: "God, may the hearts of our blended family be open to receiving one another. Just as you have adopted us as your children, may the members of our stepfamily adopt one another as family."

Scripture confirms, in Romans 8:14, that those who are led by the Spirit are sons and daughters of God. God has opened his heart toward us in mercy and loving-kindness. So pray that the members of your home will also open their hearts to one another. Ask for a spirit of mercy and loving-kindness to permeate your home.

It is awesome to be adopted by God. And it's awesome to adopt one another in love.

> *Loving Father, thank you for adopting us to be your dearly loved children. Just as you opened your heart to us, we ask you to open the hearts of our family members and draw us toward one another in love.*

A Hill Worth Dying On

When kids alternate between two homes, you can't expect to win every single parenting battle. But yes, there are some issues that do represent a hill worth dying on. Single parents and blended-family parents know that they can't control how the other home parents the children—and really they shouldn't try. But what do you do when there's an unhealthy influence in that other environment?

Trying to live at peace does mean making accommodations from time to time, but not every time. So start here: Before engaging the conflict, decide together with your spouse which issues are worth the battle and how you can best proceed to address the problem. Doing this will protect your marriage and help the two of you brace for impact. Then, use respect and tact as you engage the other home.

Remember, the battle is for your child's well-being, not necessarily for yours.

> *Help me recognize when it's time to go to battle on behalf of my child, and teach me how to confront others with thoughtfulness and respect.*

Take a Radical Road Trip

Sometimes stepfamily relationships need a kick in the seat of the pants! And here's an idea to do just that: If the developing relationships in your family have stalled—if they aren't deepening any more—try a radical road trip. In the book *The Smart Stepfamily*, I share how taking my family to Ghana each year to work with rescued trafficked children has drawn us all together and deepened our trust in God.

If throwing the football or exchanging text messages is not cutting it, then it's time you dive deep into a service project or mission trip. Facing new and uncomfortable challenges together—*together*—can break through barriers and deepen your relationships. At the same time, the experience will be connecting you to what God really cares about and deepening your relationship with him as well.

It won't be cheap or convenient. But it might just be the best therapy you ever had.

Lord, push us out of our individual comfort zones into a challenge or project that will allow us to serve you while drawing closer to each other.

What Not to Do in Parenting

earning to be a good parent, in part, means knowing what *not* to do. Have you ever felt clueless as a parent? Yes, of course you have. Everyone does—myself included. It's really tempting in those moments to fall back on criticism or name-calling. Or you may feel like yelling at or pleading with the child. And then there's the threat-repeating parent who keeps on saying, "You better not, or else . . ." The problem is, there's never an "or else"—just empty threats that train the child to ignore the parent.

Now, here's the thing: All of these strategies might seem to change the child's immediate behavior, but none of them are effective in the long run. Even worse, over time they defeat your child's spirit and ruin your authority as a parent. This is especially true in the case of stepparents.

So take some time to learn about good parenting and stepparenting. The next generation is depending on us.

Lord, I ask you to help me prayerfully examine my parenting habits and point out any that might hurt my child or our relationship in the long run.

Listen with Empathy

If you have any relationships that are important to you, or people you care about, I want to give you a principle that will strengthen those relationships. Are you listening? No, I don't mean, "Are you waiting to hear my advice?" I mean, "Are you listening to the people who are important to you?" To be specific, I want to know if you are listening *empathetically* in order to discern their needs.

Here's an example to show why this is so important: Stepmom Sara needs her kitchen to be clean and orderly. Stepdaughter Kari set out to bake a gift for Sara. Upon discovering the messy kitchen, Sara laid into Kari for making a mess. Sadly, Sara let her need for cleanliness get in the way of identifying Kari's need to be accepted by her—not to mention her desire to do something nice for her. If Sara had been listening empathetically for Kari's need, she would have ignored the mess and thanked Kari for her kindness.

Don't be a pathetic listener; be an empathetic listener. Listen for *their* need and respond in love.

Father, instead of assuming I know another person's motivation,
help me listen with empathy so I can truly understand them.

October 16

Pray for Gentleness

Exasperate is not a word we use much today, but it means "to provoke someone to anger." Think about this: Whom do you tend to exasperate? In Ephesians 6, the Bible specifically tells fathers not to exasperate their children. The passage urges dads to instead treat children with dignity so they will grow to know the Lord. "Take them by the hand," it says, "and lead them in the way of the Master" (v. 4 THE MESSAGE paraphrase).

Sometimes in a blended family, stepchildren and stepparents exasperate each other. Usually not on purpose, of course. It's just that everyone is trying to figure out their new life under one roof. So encourage everyone in your home—kids and adults alike—not to provoke one another to anger. Maybe you could say this prayer together:

> *Lord, give the stepparents in our home a spirit of gentleness so they will not embitter children. Give stepchildren a basic respect for the stepparent's authority, and give both a soft heart for the other, that it may go well with everyone in our home.*

Don't Be So Defensive!

R eally good parents give great advice—to each other.

In order to be a good team, whenever one of you makes an observation that could help the other parent, be sure to share it. Not in a condescending or condemning fashion, but in a constructive way. Sometimes it might be about an undesirable quality or behavior in your spouse that needs to change. We all know that can be a delicate situation, but healthy parents give each other permission to speak gently into one another's lives. Why? So they can raise godly kids.

Now, here's the trap for stepfamily couples to avoid: To the biological parent, advice can feel like criticism of their child, and to the stepparent it can feel like rejection and distrust. So both of you—please don't get so defensive. Don't be afraid to hear what the other person has to say. This, in turn, will mean you can help each other even when it's necessary to broach difficult subjects. After all, that's what great parents do.

Help us learn to support each other by giving and receiving constructive feedback with the proper spirit of humility and grace.

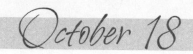

Be Long-Suffering

We all know that divorce is hard on kids, right? But did you know that on average, it takes children longer to adjust to a parent's remarriage than it does for them to adjust to a divorce? I once had a conversation with a young woman about to turn thirty years old who told me her mom had been remarried for just a couple of years. "I really love my stepdad at this point," she explained, "although early on I was completely against him." Then she added, "But please understand, it wasn't *him* I was against—it was the *idea of him* I had to get used to."

You know, when the ingredients of a blended family are thrown together, sometimes stepparents have to remember that what feels to them like resistance or rejection is not that at all. It's really just adjustment. It's not personal. It's simply a reaction to more change. Your best response is to be long-suffering and have lots of grace for one another.

Lord, give me patience as I wait for relationships to develop naturally, and discernment to recognize when rejection is not really rejection.

Living in the Land of Normal

Travel to a foreign land and you'll soon realize what you consider normal. Crossing into a different culture makes you recognize all the things you typically take for granted. I'm referring to what you consider normal in terms of language, culture, and relationships.

But don't forget, there's a flip side to this: People who have a different normal sometimes have a hard time understanding you and your ways.

Guess what? The same thing applies to family types, too. If you live in a blended family, you need to find others who also live in a stepfamily. You need to be able to talk shop about life with people who really get what your family is going through. If you talk about life with those in a first family, you might end up feeling a bit abnormal, even if you're good friends with them.

So go out and find others who live in Stepfamily Land like you do. Then you just might discover that your family is—well, pretty normal.

Heavenly Father, help each one of us avoid the comparison game as we live and thrive in Stepfamily Land.

The Hovering Parent

Hovering, overbearing parents are successful—at squashing their kids. Parents who constantly hover, sometimes called "helicopter parents," are usually anxious for their kids so they stay on top of them. "When are you going to get your homework done?" "Did you take out the trash yet?" "I've told you a hundred times—you have to manage your time better."

Now, although they're trying to teach responsibility, the message that hovering parents actually send is "You're not capable, so I have to help you." This is debilitating for kids. And when it comes from a stepparent, it also closes the door on their developing relationship.

If you really want to build up a child, get off their back. Let them make choices and experience natural consequences without your constant direction and interference. To be a more successful parent, coach from the side, not from on top.

Lord, I admit to having many concerns for my child's safety and well-being. But help me step back enough so they can go through the process of learning about choices and natural consequences.

You Can't Have It Both Ways

Hey parents, you can't have it both ways! Have you ever been the recipient of a double message from someone? You know, like when a friend tells you it's okay that you didn't call them, but then acts mad that you didn't call them. You wonder, "Well, which one is it?" It's so confusing. One trap like this in stepfamily parenting is when a biological parent claims to want the stepparent to be a part of the parenting process, but then undercuts their decisions or authority.

This is really confusing—for everyone involved. And it's defeating to stepparents. But you can't have it both ways. You can't invite someone to assume the role of co-parent in your household and then work to make them powerless and ineffective. Either they're part of the team or they're not. My suggestion is that you make them part of the team. Because that's the one way that everybody wins.

As we parent together, help me support my spouse not just with words, but with my attitude, my behavior, and my prayers.

Be Vulnerable

Want a great suggestion for deepening a friendship? It starts with *you* sharing *you.*

Ever notice that when someone is transparent and shares a vulnerability about themselves, we tend to respect them a little more? We admire their courage, and we feel like they're more approachable—like it's safe to be close to them. We also feel like we can trust them with our own vulnerabilities. And when both people share their real selves, the relationship takes a leap forward.

Now think about this: Stepfamily members can do the same thing. I've watched adult stepchildren share something personal about themselves with a parent's new spouse, and somehow it opens the door to friendship. I've also seen stepparents endear their stepkids to them just by sharing a story about a hard life lesson they learned in their younger days, or one of their most embarrassing moments.

Sure, it takes courage to put yourself out there. But courage is where great relationships begin.

Father, help me be courageous enough to allow my loved ones to see my real self.

Lead with Love

When a child misbehaves, make sure you lead with love—even though that probably won't be your first instinct.

Jaylen found out that his teenage stepson had intimidated and cussed out his mother. Now, what Jaylen really felt like doing was unloading on the kid who had mistreated his wife so badly. Instead, he took a different approach.

With great compassion and a calm tone, Jaylen asked the young man what prompted him to be disrespectful. You see, he chose to open the conversation with a question, not a statement. That got the young man reflecting on himself and his behavior instead of automatically getting defensive and making excuses. The son eventually recognized how out of line he was. And the more he talked, the more apologetic he became.

Then, and only then, did Jaylen lean across the table, look the young man in the eye, and sternly tell him never to treat his mother like that again.

When I'm tempted to lash out or dump my frustrations on someone, remind me to open the conversation with words that allow love to lead the way to understanding and respect.

A Loaded Question

Are we family, or are we not?"

The Bible makes it clear that God is relational. And since we're created in his image, we have a deep need for connection. Finding a sense of belonging, being loved, and giving love—with God and with others—are among the deepest longings of our souls. So it's no surprise that when a child can't win a parent's approval . . . if a person feels unaccepted by their peers . . . if a spouse feels unimportant to their partner . . . or when a stepcouple feels like their family isn't coming together, anxiety and fear set in.

The question "Am I important to you?" is loaded with insecurity. Now, here's the irony: That question adds to what gets in the way of finding connection in the first place. It's much better, but more difficult, to act on the basis of your love for another person than it is to worry about how much they love you. When we live that way, we'll be imitating God: "We love because he first loved us" (1 John 4:19).

Heavenly Father, in every relationship give me the courage to be the first one to love.

Truth Brings Freedom

an you imagine this man's surprise? He thought he was her fifth husband, but two years into their marriage, he found out he was her ninth! She had lied because she was afraid that he wouldn't marry her if he knew the whole story. But here's the problem with that mindset: Lying—and hiding part of the truth—just means you have to live in fear, every day.

The issue here is your integrity and trustworthiness. Lying about your past creates an artificial foundation for your relationship that will feel fragile, not stable. Well into the marriage you'll probably start feeling anxious; that's assuming you didn't experience that the day you took your vows. You'll live each day fearful that if your spouse ever finds out the truth, you're sunk.

Yes, being honest may cost you something, but it's better in the long run to have a relationship built on truth than on quicksand. Because we know what a dangerous foundation that would be.

Lord, teach me the joy of living with such honesty and integrity before you and others that I never need to waste time worrying about being exposed.

Play!

Here's a not-so-secret quality of strong families: They have fun together! As I said, it's not some big, profound secret, but it's still worth talking about. Playing together as a family lightens everyone's mood, allows you to share fun and joy, and creates wonderful memories that strengthen your family's foundation. And for stepfamilies, there's a bonus positive impact: It bonds hearts together.

Dividing up into teams, playing games together, and having a little friendly competition can help break down walls and forge new depths in step-relationships. But then, so does reading a book together, learning to play an instrument, sharing your love of movies or music, or going on a family hike in the great outdoors.

Sure, there will be times when not everyone wants to engage in every activity. But find out what your family members do like, and then take it one day at a time. As much as you can, get out there and play!

Father, remind us not to neglect the relationship-building power of simply letting our hair down and having fun together as a family.

Obey the Law of Love

So, let me get this straight. I'm expected to raise my stepchildren, provide for them, and pay for their education, but I don't have any legal rights to them?"

Yep, you got that right. Your life investment in them is not protected under the law. That seems strange and unfair, doesn't it? But the answer to this dilemma is not legal—it's relational.

You see, *love* would sacrifice financially and not worry about a return on investment. *Love* would willingly commit time and energy to the stepkids' care despite knowing that, should the biological parent die, you could be pushed out of the family picture. And *love* would lift up God's law to a child even though man's law acts like you don't exist. Why? The answer can be found in 1 Corinthians 13:8: Because "love never fails" (NASB).

Father, help me be the best parent I can be without giving thought to what I might get in return. I ask you to permanently imprint my love on the hearts of my children, regardless of what might happen in the future.

Be Like a Hall Monitor

New stepparents who are wise function like old-fashioned hall monitors: They know what's going on, but they aren't always a part of it.

Eager stepparents have the best of intentions, but sometimes they tend to plunge right into the middle of a child's life too quickly. Wise is the stepparent who monitors rather than diving in during those early days. They know the child's schedule and periodically check in with them about band practice and other activities. They ask about friends, the upcoming math test, and what the child wants for Christmas.

But they don't step into the child's personal life, feelings, and concerns . . . until they are invited in. You see, you have to take a small step before you can take a bigger step.

So hang in there and wait for your opening. Maybe right now you feel like you're nothing more than a chauffeur, but trust me, it won't be like that forever.

Lord, give me patience as I learn how to show interest in my stepchild without making them feel pressured and as I wait for their invitation to fully step into their life.

Redeeming the Next Generation

For kids, a healthy stepfamily is a great blessing. We've known for years that divorce leaves a negative emotional residue on a child's heart that can be witnessed over time. Two examples of this negative impact are cohabiting as adults and having a higher divorce rate than kids who grow up in intact families. But thankfully, that's not the end of the story.

Research now confirms that a healthy stepfamily not only prevents another divorce in a child's life, but it gives them a healthy model of marital relationships that equips them for marriage as adults.[26] In other words, after divorce a strong, stable, healthy stepfamily lowers the divorce rate in this generation *and* in the next. It reverses the curse.

What Satan tries to destroy through divorce, God can take back in just one generation.

When you're having a bad day, hang on to that good news and keep going.

God, please touch our family with your redeeming power and help us prepare and equip our children for future healthy marriages of their own.

Dress Up in Virtue

When you woke up today, you got to decide what clothes you wanted to put on, didn't you? (That's assuming you're older than age two, in which case someone else probably chose for you. Or maybe not.) Colossians 3:12, 14 tells us to "Put on . . . compassionate hearts, kindness, humility, meekness, and patience. . . . And above all these, put on love."

Just as you choose your clothes every morning, you make a conscious decision whether or not to wear those virtues as you go throughout your day. And when you do put them on, you get the chance to reflect Jesus to your spouse, your children, your co-workers, your friends, and to the world. Now it might not feel natural at first, but the more you wear these clothes, the better they start to fit you.

So go on—get them out of the closet and get dressed for heaven's sake. (Pun intended!)

Father, help me remember to begin each day by choosing to slip on the perfect outfit you've selected for me as described in Colossians 3.

The Ghost of Insecurity

Ghosts . . . can make you really insecure. "Ron, my ghost keeps telling me that my second husband will abandon me just like the first one did—that I won't be enough for him, and that he will always consider the mother of his children to be his first concern."

Yes, ghosts can make us feel insecure. They can cause us to grow fearful that we're second place to someone else. But when do you start counting? This woman assumed her husband's first wife was really his first love, but couldn't his first love have been his first romance? His first high school sweetheart? I mean, how often are we actually *the first*?

Perhaps what's needed is confidence—confidence in yourself as a person of worth and in your spouse's commitment to you. Live as if all of that is true, and you just may bust your ghost.

> *Help us chase away any ghosts of insecurity by having an unshakable trust and confidence in ourselves, in each other, and most of all, in you as our Savior and Protector of our marriage.*

Get on the Same Page

Every blended family is a cross-cultural experience. When you think about it, you're essentially merging two cultures. Language, traditions, inside jokes, the meaning we attach to certain words and actions. . . . The list could go on. And merging parenting expectations is part of this as well. For example, he always made his kids pick up their toys before coming to the dinner table. She let her kids clean them up after dinner. So who's right? Which style should they adopt as they merge the two cultures into one?

Actually, I don't know the answer. I've searched the Scriptures and can't find a single passage about clean-up time. What I *can* tell you is this: For the sake of your marriage and your family, the most important thing is that you both end up on the same side. So go ahead and talk, negotiate, and share your perspectives. In the end, choose a path you will both support. And then you'll have the right answer for your family.

Father, keep us patient, considerate, and willing to compromise as we move through the process of blending our two cultures into a single, united identity for our family.

Take a Time-Out

If you want to *feel* close in your marriage, then *do* things that make you close. This isn't rocket science, you know. There are a lot of demands calling out for our time and attention every day. But healthy couples realize that it's up to them to make day-to-day decisions that protect their time together. And they do something proactive with that time to nurture their relationship.

I'm talking about *talking* together. Just the two of you. No cell phones, no television, no kids, no social media. Actual talking. About your day, your concerns, your parenting, your faith—about you and about each other. And doing things together helps your closeness, too, especially for stepcouples. Ninety-four percent of happy couples in stepfamilies have hobbies and interests that bring them together, and ninety-four percent said togetherness was a top priority for them.

So don't forget: The couple that plays together, stays together. Now go schedule some special time with your spouse.

Lord, in the busyness of our lives, never let us forget to set aside time dedicated to the two of us to nurture our special relationship.

November 3

Don't Chase Their Approval

Sometimes stepparents find themselves at a real disadvantage. Now this might sound off track at first, but here's a posture I wish all parents would adopt: Don't care too much about winning your kids' approval. You see, chasing their approval puts you in a position of weakness. It makes you hesitate when you need to set a boundary. It causes you to waver when you should come down hard on their misbehavior. So ironically, not caring too much puts you in a position of strength.

This is also why stepparents, who on some level *are* chasing a child's acceptance, find themselves at a disadvantage in parenting. And that's why they need the biological parent to be the "heavy" in the beginning of the marriage, so they can be free to focus more on bonding with the kids.

Yes, it's a disadvantage for stepparents. But teamwork will get you through and make your family stronger in the end.

Heavenly Father, please help me learn to parent in ways that will earn my children's respect, not necessarily their approval of my decisions.

Role with the Changes

Parents have to "role" with the changes.

A biological parent's role changes over time. As a child grows in maturity and responsibility we shift from *telling* young children, to *teaching* adolescents, to *delegating* or *coaching* young adults.

A stepparent's role might shift from being a *babysitter* (who with borrowed power enforces the parent's rules), to an *aunt* or *uncle* (who is like a trusted extended family member), to a *bonus parent* (who has lots of relational equity and the authority that comes with it). Those who become stepparents later in life likely start and finish in a *friend* or *mentor* role with their adult stepchildren.

How your role changes depends on you and the child—and it can be confusing. So check in periodically with your spouse to see how they view things. And try to relax and enjoy the relationship you currently have. It may not be everything you hope for, but skipping over what you have while trying to get what you want will only make you unhappy. Find contentment and joy in whatever role you're called to play.

For today, God, give me the wisdom and grace to fill my role to the best of my ability.

Pots of Money

So, how many pots of money do you have? Yes, I know—you don't have any actual pots of money lying around. But you do probably have a bank account. And you have line items in your budget that you put money in.

Couples in first marriages generally have one pot of money. They deposit their income and pay all their bills out of that joint account, and they co-own their assets. But couples in stepfamilies use a variety of money systems. They might have one joint account. Or they might designate two that represent the assets or obligations of each partner. Other couples have three pots: a *his*, a *hers*, and an *ours*.

Your system or style of money management doesn't really matter that much. But what does matter is that you both agree to the system, and that you base it on God's values about spending, saving, and providing for your kids.

Lord, we desire to honor you by being good stewards of our money and resources. Show us the plan that will work best for our family and be based on your values.

This Is Bigger than You

What? Cards, gifts, and acts of kindness—for your ex-spouse? Yes, as a matter of fact, you read that right.

Did you hear about the guy who took flowers, cards, and a gift to his children so they could give them to his ex-wife? And that's not all, he then helped his kids cook her breakfast.

When pressed for an explanation of his kindness and generosity, he answered, "I'm raising two little men. The example I set in how I treat their mom is going to significantly shape how they see and treat women. . . . I think even more so in my case because we are divorced. So if you aren't modeling good relationship behavior for your kids, get your [act] together. I don't care if [they don't deserve it]. Rise above it and be an example. This is bigger than you."

All I can add to that is "Amen!"

Help me set aside any pettiness and ill feelings toward my ex-spouse so I can model godly behavior that will impact my children's character development in positive ways.

Slow Down Your Dating

Sometimes kids just don't listen. And parents? Sometimes they don't listen so well either.

After dating a seventy-year-old man for just three and a half months, Tina's mom, aged sixty-seven, announced her plans to marry him. Tina, her siblings, and the grandchildren, along with the kids and grandkids on the other side, were all asking the couple to slow down, but they just wouldn't listen.

Now imagine the shoe is on the other foot. Let's say your child is making an expensive or impulsive decision. You'd want them to listen to your advice, right? So be sure to always take the pulse of your family and trusted advisors. If there's a consensus that you're moving too fast, then slow down your dating or your plans for marriage.

Basically, you have two choices: You can resent them and move forward without them, or you can pause, listen, and take them along with you.

Father, in every relationship and every decision, help me move at the speed that fits your timetable for my life.

Appropriately Sad

One of the ways we help children grieve well is by making them pick up their socks. I know that sounds strange, but think about what typically happens. A big temptation for parents of a grieving child is to go soft on them—which is perfectly understandable. Life has thrown them a curve (or two). They've been through a lot, and you ache for them.

But you can't let that keep you from holding them responsible for their behavior. If you do, they'll learn pretty quickly that sadness is a powerful tool that lets them get away with stuff. Ephesians 4:26 suggests that we can be angry and not sin. In other words, we are still responsible to manage our behavior even when feeling bad. I think we can make the same application with sadness.

Yes, be sympathetic for the struggles your children have endured. Hug their sadness away whenever you can. But at the same time, hold them accountable for their behavior. Help them learn to be sad in appropriate ways, and responsible in how they live.

Lord, when my child is sad or grieving, help me strike the right balance between sensitivity to their pain and firmness in teaching them responsibility.

Softened Hearts

Have you ever been on the outside looking in? It's not much fun, is it? Maybe it was junior high when you wanted to belong to that group of kids so badly, but they just wouldn't let you in. Or maybe it was a social club in college, or a church softball team, or a prestigious professional organization—whenever it happened, it's just never any fun being on the outside.

What does it take for a group of insiders to allow an outsider in? It requires softened hearts. When it comes to a stepfamily, biological family members (the insiders) have to soften their hearts to make room for the new members (the outsiders). Yep, all those insiders, including grandparents, former in-laws, aunts, and uncles—everyone has to choose to open up their heart and welcome the new members.

So when you pray for your family, ask for softened and open hearts in everyone involved. Let love in and see what happens.

Loving Father, keep the hearts of every member of our family softened and responsive toward each other, and most of all, toward you.

Three Powerful Words

Here's a pop quiz for you men: What are the three little words every woman longs to hear? Did you answer, *I love you*? If so, you're wrong. Of course, the words *I love you* are pretty special and represent music to a woman's ears. But so are these words: *Tell me more.*

If you men are confused at this point, let me explain: To a woman, *Tell me more* is *not* about getting more facts or detailed information. No, to the woman you love, those three words communicate these messages: "I care about you," "I'm interested in what you think, and feel, and what matters to you," and most important, "I'm with you—we're connected."

Contrast that to my goof-up moment when I interrupted my wife in the middle of her story to ask a totally unrelated question. Yes, I had to work to repair that one. Next time I'm going to try listening with my eyes and really tuning in. "Tell me more about that, Babe."

Lord, help us communicate caring to each other by our eagerness to share and listen.

A Readiness to Sacrifice

Courage . . . means a strong desire to live taking the form of readiness to die."

G. K. Chesterton made that statement in reference to November 11, Veterans Day. And rightfully so. Throughout history, men and women of great courage have adopted a readiness to die in order that we might live. And for that, we are eternally grateful.

In a battle of a different kind, I have seen courageous people displaying the readiness to die to self in order that others might benefit:

- Men and women who daily sacrifice their personal desires in order to serve their spouse and live at peace with one another
- Stepparents who fight for the well-being of children not their own
- Children who overcome barriers to bravely love stepsiblings and stepparents
- And parents who shield their home from the arrows of the Evil One

This Veterans Day, let's celebrate both the courage of those who have fought for our country and those who fight for our homes.

Just as you laid down your life for me, Jesus, give me greater courage to love my children with a sacrificial love that always acts in their best interests.

Spy Kids

It may be a lot of fun to watch spy movies, but if you're a co-parent with kids living between two homes, never ask them to become a spy kid for you.

When my kids were young they enjoyed the movie *Spy Kids*. It's about the children of secret-agent parents who have to become spies themselves in order to rescue their parents from danger. Fun premise for a story, but never ask your child to do that in real life.

Questions like "What did you do at their house this weekend?" "Is your dad still dating that woman?" and "How can she afford to give you that?" may seem harmless, but they end up forcing your child into a loyalty bind that can make them feel guilty for liking or loving their other parent or family members. And believe me, that hurts your child.

Don't try to turn your children into spy kids. Instead, give your permission for them to love others. And you take care of yourself.

Help me be careful never to put my kids in a position where they feel forced to choose between loyalties to different homes or family members.

Ditch the Shame

There's a shame virus infecting parents, and it's past time we address the issue.

Parents love their kids. But they don't always have the same affection or measure of delight for each child. Parents often whisper this truth to me in shame and guilt, fearful that they're the only ones who feel that way. In fact, I hear such comments on a consistent basis.

I hear it from biological parents who don't relate well to the interests of one child—or don't like who their adult child has become. And from adoptive parents and stepparents who are still bonding with a child and struggling to work out their relationship.

Hey, feeling differently about kids is normal. It's okay. Just do your best to treat them fairly and with kindness. Work at becoming more empathetic. And ask God to grow your love over time. You may not feel about them today as you'd like, but tomorrow is a new day.

Lord, help me accept the fact that I won't feel the exact same emotions with all of my children. Show me how to make each one feel equally valued.

Improve Your Parenting

When it comes to parenting, don't forget that united you stand, but divided *they* fall. What I mean by that is that parents who don't agree on how to parent soon discover that their kids are the ones who suffer most from the divisiveness. The kids fall through the cracks, get caught in the crossfire of battles, or react to the stress with countless negative behaviors. This is especially true in blended families because couples naturally start out on day one with a few undefined gaps in their parenting. If you don't work to overcome that, you just might stay stuck that way.

One thing that can help unify you is learning good parenting skills and techniques. Read a book together, take a class, watch a video series, join a small group—there's lots of quality parent training available to choose from. You really have no excuse to stay divided. So stop the arguing. Getting on the same parenting page bridges your gaps, protects the well-being of your children, and strengthens your home in countless ways.

Father God, lead us to the right resources that can help us work together as a team to grow into better parents.

Don't Become a Hostage

Try not to let somebody hold your parenting hostage. Single parents and stepfamily parents know that the parenting that occurs in their child's other home can affect how they themselves parent. If parents in the other home buy the kids things, it can make you feel like you have to buy them things, too. And if they say yes to something you've already said no to, you may find yourself rethinking and second-guessing your own decisions. Pretty soon the fear of what an ex might do can paralyze you.

Pray for courage to press in and carry on despite what the other home is doing. And fight the temptation to try to undo their influence. You just focus on keeping a balanced attitude and practicing good parenting. And trust that providing consistent boundaries and love will, in the end, make all the difference to your kids. Because it will.

Lord, help me make the best decisions for my child and not be swayed by how others might choose to parent in a different way.

Always Second, Never First

Sharing special occasions for the first time with someone we love is part of what makes the relationship special. But what if your *first* is their *second*? Sometimes second spouses are envious of all the "firsts" they missed out on. Michelle admitted to me that she felt jealous of the fact that her first child would be her husband's third. "Every little thing is so special to me," she said. "But it's old hat for him. I feel like we are in two different places and that I'm never first—I'm always going to be second."

Yes, it's true that her husband is going to react differently to things that he's already experienced. But that doesn't mean Michelle is going to be second in his heart.

Whether you're a wife or a husband struggling with the "second-place blues," don't allow your fears to tell you how you rank with somebody else. Instead, pay attention to the actions and choices of your spouse. That should convince you that in their eyes, you're number one.

Father, take our focus off past relationships so we can enjoy every experience we share as if it were fresh and new to both of us.

Listening Is Good for Your Heart

We see a lot of advice these days about protecting our heart health—and for good reason. We need our hearts to function properly, pumping blood to keep the other systems in our body working. It's also vital to protect the heart of our marriage so that family relationships function smoothly. One way to do that: Be a really good listener. Listening is one of the most important and, honestly, one of the most difficult skills of marriage. You wouldn't think so because we all talk and listen to dozens of people and media outlets every day.

I think what's hard is listening beneath your spouse's words to how they feel, and working to understand what the statement really means to *them*. All this, while being careful not to make assumptions and not to listen through a filter of what their words mean to *you*. Listening is costly. Everyone has something to say, but really good lovers discipline themselves to listen instead.

You can strengthen your heart—and your mate's—by learning to be a better listener.

Lord, teach me how to listen so that I understand what my spouse is really saying.

Stay on Topic

Here's an important message for co-parents: For the sake of your kids, find a way to do business with each other. You're no longer together as husband and wife, but you're still raising your kids together. An atmosphere of cooperation between homes is a must for your children's emotional stability. Unfortunately, that's often tough to establish when your personal relationship has been broken in the past.

But that broken relationship points toward the key to cooperating well: Talk about parental things, not personal ones. Parental topics include Johnny's health, school matters, and managing his social media time—they *don't* include personal issues like why you got divorced or whose fault it was. Learn to separate old marital pain from current parental matters so you can stay on task and not resurrect conflict.

Ask God to help you set aside your past emotional baggage and your personal agenda so the two of you can be the best team you can be—for Johnny's sake.

> *Help me learn ways to effectively communicate with other significant people in my children's lives so that we focus on ways to ensure their well-being.*

Before You Travel

When the cat's away, the mice will . . . try to play the other parent, that's what! In lots of families, one parent has to travel from time to time. It might be a business trip, a visit to a distant family member, or a military deployment. And sometimes, at least one kid tries to play the parent who's been left in charge. This used to happen to my wife whenever I traveled to speak at conference events.

So what can you do to ease the situation? We figured out a couple of things that helped: First and foremost, make sure that you're on the same page about household rules. And remember to communicate to the kids that the remaining parent is fully in charge, and that you expect their complete cooperation. This is especially important in stepfamilies when the biological parent is the one leaving the home to travel. After that, stand your ground and follow through.

> *Heavenly Father, please help us train our children to respect our authority and to understand that we expect the same behavior from them whether we are present or not.*

What Do I Call You?

There's some disagreement and confusion about the best term to refer to a stepfamily. And sometimes members of a stepfamily are confused about what to call *each other*.

Whenever you marry into a family, you have to figure out what to call your extended family members. Sometimes you call your mother-in-law Mom, and sometimes you don't. And sometimes you grow into it later.

The same holds true for blended families. Is it Stepmom or Mom? The trick is for the stepparent and stepchildren to figure it out together. Try asking questions of each other like, "What term do you find yourself using the most?" "How would you like to be introduced in public settings or with friends?" and "At home, what term feels most comfortable for you?" It will probably take a while to settle the matter, but taking everyone's opinions into consideration is a good first step.

These questions will help you understand and honor one another's preferences—which ultimately will make you feel more like family.

Lord, help me set aside my preconceived ideas about labels and take the time to learn what makes other family members feel most comfortable.

A Cycle of Gratitude

Did you know that there's a cycle of gratitude? It goes like this: When you are grateful to God, it changes who you are to those around you. Think about it—when your heart is full of gratitude to God for all he has done for you, a little of your thankfulness can't help but spill over to those around you in the form of kindness and mercy.

Then, as 2 Corinthians 9:12–15 tells us, your generosity results in *them* giving thanks to God. Other people will "glorify God" because of *your* obedience to him, and because of the grace of God that is so evident within *you*. So your thankfulness to God produces kindness toward others, which produces in them gratitude to God. And so the cycle continues on.

You have the power to ignite this cycle of gratitude (or recycling) any time you want. Think about that while you get ready to have a happy Thanksgiving!

Father, use me to be a blessing to those around me by keeping me mindful of the many blessings you have lavished on me.

Thank God for Your Family

"Enter his gates with thanksgiving, and his courts with praise!" (Psalm 100:4).

No, the writer of Psalm 100 was not referencing the national holiday we know as Thanksgiving. He was talking about coming before the Lord with a heart of gratitude and praise. He continues: "Give thanks to him; bless his name! For the Lord is good; his steadfast love endures forever, and his faithfulness to all generations" (vv. 4–5).

During your Thanksgiving celebration this year, be sure to pause between bites of turkey and pumpkin pie to express your deep gratitude to the Lord who is faithful to all generations and whose love endures forever. And then, tell him how grateful you are for each member of your family. Express your appreciation for the fact that he has brought you together. Oh, and then be sure to tell your family that you thanked God for them.

After that, you can get back to that pumpkin pie.

Father, may a spirit of praise and gratitude for your goodness be at the heart of our Thanksgiving celebration this year.

Become the Spouse You Need to Be

Are you becoming the spouse you need to be? Gail wrote to our ministry expressing appreciation for the training and resources we offer. Then she said something that caught my attention: "Clearly, divorce is not part of God's design for marriage. But when you have divorced and are remarried, that is all the more reason to make sure you now become the spouse you need to be."

Gail doesn't want to repeat her past history. And so, with her new insights about marriage, she is moving herself toward becoming the spouse she needs to be. Not what other women might be called to, and not some image of the perfect wife our culture puts out there. Gail is working toward a specific goal: to become who and what she needs to be in *her* marriage, for *her* husband, in *this* blended family.

Blooming where you're planted—that's always a good idea.

Lord, please grow me into the best spouse and the best parent for this family, for this point in time.

Keep an Open Mind

Here's another simple but crucial step for managing holiday stress: Be flexible. This tip is especially important for newly formed step-families because everyone has their own ideas about what to serve at Thanksgiving, how to decorate for Christmas, and what to wear on St. Patrick's Day! Believe me, you don't realize just how firmly you hold to your traditions until someone else wants to change things. And that's when people get stubborn. "What do you mean eat ham at Thanksgiving? That's not how we do it around here."

Being flexible recognizes that you can retain some traditions while you'll need to modify, combine, or completely drop others—all while trying to invent new traditions to go with your new family. Honestly, for many blended families finding agreement and making everyone happy takes years. So be patient, humble, and flexible—and eventually you'll get there.

Help us all be respectful of the different ideas and traditions each family member brings to the table. Guide us as we plan celebrations that the whole family can enjoy and feel a part of.

Build New Traditions

When it comes to traditions, the best approach is to borrow from the past while creating something in the present. Every newly married couple knows that it's important to honor some of the traditions you grew up with even as you create your own new family traditions. New stepfamilies have the same task, but it's a little more complicated since a lot more people are invested in the process.

Here's one tip to consider: Decide on a new tradition; then try it and see what happens.

Be sure to get your family together before the event and let everyone share their expectations. Then decide on a plan and implement it. If it doesn't go well, you've still learned something. At least next time you'll be better informed.

If it does go well, you've gained a new tradition and everyone contributed to the process. And doesn't that sound like a family being born?

Father, help us come together as a family to adopt new traditions that are meaningful to everyone, that honor our past while looking ahead to the future.

As Long as It Takes

Here's a pop quiz on a familiar biblical story: How long did the father wait for the prodigal son to return? (See Luke 15:11–24.) I often ask the parents of prodigal children that question. It's a trick question, really, because the answer is he waited as long as it took. I make the same point whenever I talk with stepparents who are trying to connect with a child who has their back turned toward them.

Now, please don't misunderstand; I know it's terribly frustrating. One stepdad told me about his twelve-year-old stepdaughter: "I tried and tried, but she never warmed up to me—so I just gave up." I asked him how long he had waited for her attitude to change. "Three months," he answered. *Three months.*

This stepdad started out on the right track; he just stopped short. The correct answer is as long as it takes. Are you willing to wait as long as it takes?

> *When I feel like giving up on one of my kids, give me the strength and perseverance to wait however long it takes for their heart to change.*

Hold Me

Here's something ironic: Sometimes, when we're feeling insecure in our marriage, we yell at our spouse so they'll come closer. (How's that been working out?) Getting negative when we really just want to be held doesn't make sense, but I think it's human nature. I know I'm that way—and a lot of the couples I counsel are, too.

It reminds me of how my dog barks at people when they come to the door, and then runs out to greet them with her teeth showing. I know all she really wants is for them to pick her up and hold her, but they think she's trying to attack.

Here's a better approach: Stop baring your teeth. And stop barking! Instead, calm yourself and present your need in a way that can be understood and received by your spouse. Say something like "I've been feeling a little disconnected lately. Any chance we could spend some time together soon?" Give that a try and see if you don't get a better response.

Lord, help us learn to express our needs to each other clearly and calmly instead of lashing out in frustration.

Replace Complaining with Contentment

Wouldn't any parent appreciate a little gratitude from their child? I thought about this the other day while running around getting the windshield fixed and some maintenance done on the car that my son drives. When I called and asked him to come pick me up, I got attitude. Apparently I had disrupted his Saturday morning sleep.

Evidently it didn't matter to him that I had gotten up at 6:15 a.m. in order to get that car fixed or that I was spending money to fix it. I was ticked. Then I started to wonder, *Does God have this same problem with me?* I have a good job that puts food on our table and provides for all my family's needs and yet I sometimes manage to find something to complain or whine about. Ouch, that insight really hurt!

All children—our children *and* God's—need to learn gratitude and how to express it. We all need to learn to be content.

Father, instead of complaining and finding fault, teach me to live out the truth of Paul's words in Philippians 4:11: "I have learned in whatever situation I am to be content."

More than Enough Love

Who do you love more? Him or us?"

Many biological parents have heard this accusing question from their kids. It usually comes when they're feeling insecure, like when your marriage is pulling you away from them (which is inherent to falling in love). So what can you do?

I suggest that biological parents respond this way: "My spouse is the most important adult in my life. You are the most important child(ren) in my life. I love you both very much. God has given me more than enough love for all of you. I love you and I will always be here for you."

Don't get caught up in grading or ranking your loves ("I love my husband just a fraction of a point more than you."). That's not the issue. Reassuring them of your love will meet their need. Say it with words, with a hug, and with a little of your time. That translates as love to them more than any ranking system.

Give me words and actions that will help my children feel secure and convince them that our family has plenty of love for everyone.

Just Not Home Anymore

I don't know. It just doesn't feel like home anymore."

That was the comment I got from a thirty-five-year-old woman as she reflected on her recent holiday visit with her family. She had gone home to the house she grew up in, but it didn't seem like the same place. Since her dad had remarried after her mom's death, she found herself surrounded by lots of new faces, and her dad was preoccupied with his wife and her family. All of that made her old home feel foreign to her.

Changes to family traditions can make children and teens feel that way, too. Which is why parents should hold on to some traditions in order to provide stability. It's also why you need to anticipate the "out-of-sorts" feeling kids commonly experience during the holidays. So go ahead and acknowledge that change is hard. Talk to them about it. And remind them that what *hasn't* changed—and never will—is your love for them.

Despite whatever changes in family relationships and holiday traditions time brings, help us always treasure and celebrate our love for each other.

Love Is a Choice

So what would you do if your fiancée told you she was pregnant and it wasn't your child?

I heard about one man who found himself in that very situation. Distraught and hurt, he chose to walk away from the mother and child. After all, the responsibilities were not his. And in the eyes of society, he had made the logical choice.

But then through a dream, the Spirit of God let Joseph know that something bigger was going on. Things were not as they seemed on the surface. And God wanted Joseph to play a key role in his plan. At that moment, Joseph made a different choice: He chose to love.

As we prepare to celebrate our dear Savior's birth this Christmas, let me applaud those of you who are stepparents (and foster parents or adoptive parents). And let me ask the biological parent in your situation to join me in honoring you because you, like Joseph, didn't have responsibilities or obligations, but chose to love anyway.

Father, help me always hold fast to the choice I made to love.
Show me how to encourage other stepparents to do the same.

Holiday Step-Stress Tip: Plan, Plan, Plan

My number one tip for dealing with step-stress during the holidays has three words: *Plan, plan, plan.* Of course, everyone has to plan for the holidays. But stepfamilies have to be even more proactive because of the complexity involved. For example, if you have two, three, or more homes to coordinate, start planning visitation and travel schedules months in advance. Don't wait until the last minute or everyone will suffer.

You may also have to plan gift giving with multiple households and grandparents so that little Johnny doesn't get the same gift three times. And you may even have to plan to be flexible. You know, in case one of the households changes their schedule at the last minute.

No, you can't plan for every single thing that might happen during the holidays. But getting out front will certainly help you not get behind.

Help us make holiday plans that will create lasting, treasured memories for each member of our family. Most of all, may our plans focus on celebrating the day and honoring you.

Was Jesus a Stepchild?

Parents, this entry is designed for your kids. Read it first to decide if you will share it with them. If your child is an adult, find a conversational way to share the sentiment of this day's reading.

Hey kids, I've got a question for you: Was Jesus a stepchild? Over the years I've asked a lot of people that question and it surprises me how many of them have never thought about it—especially kids growing up in a stepfamily. But think about it: Jesus was raised by his mother and his stepdad, Joseph.

It's true that the circumstances surrounding his birth were definitely different from any other blended family situation. But still, if you have a stepparent or have a friend who does, you can consider Jesus someone who very much understands what it's like to be in a stepfamily.

How cool is that? You have a friend who has "been there, done that," as we say.

So talk to him (we call it praying). Tell him your joys, frustrations, worries, and concerns.

He's listening. And he will always understand your heart.

Jesus, thank you for always being ready to listen to me when I need you.

Honor the Past and the Present

Wise stepparents honor their stepchildren's past. When Victoria married a widower with four kids, she applied this advice and it really paid off. Victoria noticed how uprooted the kids seemed to feel when her furniture was moved into their family home. So she made changes very cautiously. First, she set up the kitchen according to her own tastes and needs, but she made sure that the mother's items were distributed or saved for each child. Then she waited five more years to redo the living room.

During the Christmas celebration seven years after her marriage, Victoria gifted each child with a photo of their family of origin *and* the current stepfamily. Now that's wisdom. She honored each child, their mom, their dad—and herself. And by encouraging her stepchildren to embrace their past, Victoria made it more likely that they will want to embrace her as a part of their future.

Father, show me ways to help my stepchildren know that I honor their past history and the other family members in their life as part of who they are.

See It from Their Point of View

Ever heard the saying "To better understand someone else, walk a mile in their shoes"? That's really good advice in a lot of situations, but it's especially helpful when it comes to dealing with difficult people. You know, that co-worker who really annoys you, or the parent at your child's school that everybody complains about. Or how about your ex-spouse, or maybe your child's stepparent in the other home?

The Bible tells us in Romans 12:18, "So far as it depends on you, live peaceably with all." One thing that can help us live in peace with each other is being empathetic. Seeing life from the other person's point of view, especially as it relates to how they interact with you, just might recalibrate your perspective of them—and yourself. Having empathy for others won't fix every dilemma, but it does remind your heart to be patient with others. And that's surely a mercy we all benefit from.

Whenever I think that someone is being difficult, Lord, please open my eyes to see things from their viewpoint, especially how they perceive my behavior and me.

You Married the Wrong Person

Have you ever felt like you married the wrong person? If you asked me if you married the wrong person, my answer would be, "Yes, you did," primarily because you were wanting the wrong things. See, in some ways, we *all* married the wrong person.[27] Think about it—you really didn't know what you needed, or what you needed to know, when you chose the one you chose. But assuming that you're willing to become who you need to become in order to love the spouse you chose, then by God's grace you'll discover you married the right person. He or she was the wrong person for who you *were* in the beginning, but they're the right person for who you're now becoming in Christ.

Yes, even when you were idealistic and confused about what you truly needed, you still picked better than you knew, someone who could love someone like you.

> *Lord, help me grow into not just the right person for my spouse, but the best one for them.*

Stepgrandparents

D o you want to know two things that go well together this time of year? Grandparents and Christmas!

When I was growing up, my family lived far away from my grandparents. The only time I got to see them was at Christmas—which was great because grandparents give awesome gifts.

Christmas is a natural time to connect the generations. Sometimes stepfamilies are still trying to figure out how to do that. For example, some stepgrandparents didn't choose that role; they fell into it because someone else decided to get married. But that doesn't mean they won't be excited about it. Still, bonding between the generations is dependent upon the motivation of the parties: the stepgrandparent, the adult child, and the stepgrandchild.

Here's the point: This Christmas take advantage of every opportunity to connect the generations. Talk. Share. Play games. After all, there are memories to be made and a Savior to celebrate and share.

Thank you for the blessing of having grandparents in our lives. Help us find ways this season to encourage deeper relationships and sharing between generations.

Give Them Choices

Parents, I have a question for you: Would you rather parent halfheartedly and hope it blesses your kids, or parent well and know for sure that it will? Did you notice what I did there? I gave you a choice. And that points to one good way to train up your children. Beginning as early as you can, give them choices, and then let them experience the blessings or difficulties those choices bring.

"Would you rather clean your room or have us pay your sister with your allowance to do it for you?" (Notice that a clean room is not an option, but the child is allowed to choose how it will happen.) "Would you rather help cook dinner or help clean up?" (Helping with dinner is a given, but how the child helps is up to them.) "Would you rather do your homework before TV time or after?" (Homework isn't optional, but the child can choose when to do it.)

Giving choices invites cooperation, increases follow-through, and trains kids to think for themselves. And all those benefits do more than just bring peace and harmony to your home; they bless your child for the rest of their life.

Father, please give us wisdom as we offer our children choices
that will develop their character and teach them responsibility.

Financing Togetherness

To pre-nup or not to pre-nup? My recommendation is to go an entirely different route.

Financial planners often encourage second-marriage and pre-stepfamily couples to get a prenuptial agreement, but those words often leave a bad taste in people's mouths. It sounds like you're planning for a divorce. How can someone already thinking ahead to a future divorce be that strongly committed to the marriage?

Fortunately, there's a much better way. A Shared Covenant Agreement helps stepfamily couples manage their daily expenses, discuss insurance and retirement solutions, and do estate planning for their children and for each other. Instead of planning for separateness, it finances togetherness. And it builds confidence in how money will be used in your complex family.

Hey, it's the Christmas season, and if you're like many couples, you're feeling a little stressed about money right now. But don't let money issues divide you. Get proactive with your money management and estate planning so you can finance togetherness. The book *The Smart Stepfamily Guide to Financial Planning*[28] may help.

> *Lord, show us ways to handle our financial planning that make us feel closer to each other and more secure about the future of our family.*

Stand Together

The old familiar adage is true: Rules without relationship lead to rebellion. If you're a foster parent, adoptive parent, or stepparent, you're probably thinking right now, "Well, that's just great. Where does that leave me?" And that's a good question.

The good news is that it *is* possible for authority to exist without a bonded relationship. But that authority does have limits. A police officer can pull you over. A boss or coach can tell you what to do. And a teacher can lay down the rules of the classroom. But children don't obey these authorities out of a deep love or admiration.

That's why it's critical for new stepparents to know their limits, focus on bonding with the kids, and work in cooperation with the biological parent concerning household rules. Stand together and you can enforce the rules. Stand alone and you just might end up . . . alone.

As members of our family bond together in love, help us work together to enforce rules based more on love and respect than on sheer authority.

Divide and Conquer

When forgiving is difficult to do, try chopping it up into pieces. Maybe I'd better explain how that works.

We know the Bible calls us to forgive just as God in Christ has forgiven us (Ephesians 4:32). However, sometimes a person is willing to forgive, but doesn't know how to *practically* accomplish it. That's especially true if the wrong done to them is so massive that the idea of forgiving seems as daunting as climbing Mount Kilimanjaro.

When that's the case, make a list of the individual aspects of the mountain—the offender's words and behavior—that you're trying to forgive. Chop it up into boulders that you can specifically pray about and offer to God one at a time. No matter how big the offense was, this often makes the act of forgiving more manageable.

Of course, the process always begins with praying for God's help to let it go. After that, crossing each individual item off the list as you release it will help you conquer the mountain.

> *I want to be obedient to you in this area, Lord, so I ask for your help in leading me step-by-step through the process of forgiving anyone who has wronged me.*

The Magic of Christmas

Ahhhh, can you feel that? It's the magic of Christmas! We often hear people use that phrase, but what exactly is the "magic of Christmas"? I mean, technically it's just another day on the calendar, the same as any other day of the year. It's not like there's extra grace or Holy Spirit power floating around.

And yet it does seem that believers and nonbelievers alike tend to be kinder, more considerate, and more selfless than at any other time of year. Maybe it's the *giving* nature of the season that softens our hearts and invites us to be more loving and Christlike. I think maybe that does qualify as magic.

All family relationships get strained occasionally. Maybe this magical season is your opportunity to offer the gift of forgiveness and to restore a relationship. A long time ago that's just what a little baby born in a manger did—and we're still celebrating two thousand years later.

Father, we ask you to soften the hearts of our family members so that we can celebrate a season of forgiveness, restoration, and renewed love.

Touch Points

When someone you care about becomes unavailable, what do you do? Most of us react by finding a way to express our hurt. We might get angry or critical, or pursue more attention from the person who seems distant. Kids do the very same things. Especially when they lose attention from a parent. When a stepfamily forms, kids often lose some connection with their parent who is understandably investing time and energy in a new marriage and family. And kids might get angry or withdraw to voice their loss.

So parents, make sure you maintain touch points with your children—that is, those little rituals that communicate love and closeness. Like a special look or phrase the two of you thought up. Or sharing a bedtime story or activity that keeps you connected. And when you can't be physically together, using technology like texting, FaceTime, or Skype to stay in touch.

Do whatever it takes to be available to your child. Because your presence matters to them—a lot.

God, please guide me as I look for ways to establish touch points with each of my children that will convince them I'm always available whenever they need me.

Keep on Trucking

A word of encouragement to stepparents: Just keep on trucking. Kids do and say a lot of things that stem from childishness or teenage confusion. That's why I love it when someone grows up a little, gains some perspective, and then reflects on what they've learned.

For example, take Jason's post to stepparents: "We are going to be angry," he said. "It doesn't matter if you're the best stepdad ever; it's not your fault. At age fifteen I just started feeling like something was wrong with me or my mom . . . and it made me mad. But don't despair [stepparents], we usually come around. So just keep on trucking, as they say, and know that you make a difference, even if your stepchild can't admit it."

Hey, you did sign up for the long haul, didn't you? So the next time you feel like you're running out of gas, remember Jason's encouragement—and just keep on trucking.

Father, even when it seems that my children aren't responding to my efforts, empower me to keep on loving, keep on giving, and keep on praying.

Accept What You Can't Change

Holidays have a way of increasing the levels of stress and tension in our homes. Here's a suggestion for dealing with that: Do what you can and accept what you can't change. I have to confess that this tip is probably the most difficult one for many co-parents to follow. After all, you've contacted the other home about upcoming holiday plans. You've been reasonable, cordial, and cooperative to the best of your ability. But they're still not willing to meet you in the middle. And that frustrates you to no end.

So what can you do? Bend where you can bend. But say no when you have to and stick to your guns when that seems best. Honor your visitation schedule arrangements. In all things, make sure to repay evil with good. And as for all the other little antagonisms, for the well-being of your kids, you may just have to grin and bear it. And trust that God will bless you for taking the high road.

Lord, help me do all I can to help the holidays go smoothly for my kids and graciously accept any frustrations that come along.

A Well-Defined Relationship

DTR or "define the relationship" is more than just a concept for dating couples. Stepparents can find it useful, too. When a relationship is just beginning, or when its nature seems to be a little vague, defining the relationship can help bring clarification. A DTR conversation helps both sides understand where the relationship stands and what each person can expect from the other.

For example, kids need to hear from their stepparent that you are *not* trying to replace their biological parent; they need to be assured that you respect the special place their parent holds in their life. This helps kids relax and receive you as another safe person in their life. You can even go a step further and promise them that if they ever feel stuck between you and their biological parent, they can tell you about it and you won't get upset.

Bottom line: You know where you fit, so that frees them to love their biological parent without concern. Isn't that a winning definition of a relationship?

Lord, rather than assume my stepchild knows my intentions, help me share my vision for our relationship in ways that make them feel safe, secure, and doubly loved.

No Cookie-Cutter Kids

Here's a holiday-inspired tip for parents and stepparents: When you make Christmas cookies this year, let it remind you that there's no such thing as cookie-cutter kids.

If your family is like ours, you enjoy making Christmas cookies, and the first step of the process is pulling out your cookie cutters in festive shapes that fit the season. Of course, each cutter makes cookies that all look alike. Unless you do something weird to the dough, you know exactly how the cookies will turn out.

One day my wife, Nan, pointed out to me that our three boys are all different in their preferences, natural strengths, and temperament. So why should we expect to parent them the same or expect them all to act alike? Our job as parents is to discover each one's God-given uniqueness, celebrate it, and fan it into flame with everything we've got.

So when it comes to kids, throw away the cookie cutters. Because each one has his or her own unique shape.

Help us discern the unique God-given design of each of our children and teach them to honor you with all their gifts, strengths, and abilities.

My Most Frustrating Question

Have you ever tried to talk someone into loving you? That doesn't work very well, does it? But sometimes we can't resist the urge to try it.

When two people marry and form a blended family, they hope their children and extended family will become a loving family to one another, treating each other with care and respect. If someone asks me how they can build a bridge to a family member who refuses to embrace the new family, that tells me their dream isn't becoming reality. And their question frustrates me because I don't have a good answer to it. How do you make someone love you who just won't do it?

What you *can* do is pursue, but don't badger. Take whatever they give you and build on it. What you *can't* do is beat yourself up for not making them love you or allow yourself to give up. Stay as close to them as they'll allow, and pray diligently while you wait for their heart to change.

Heavenly Father, give us plenty of tact and patience as we wait for all of our loved ones to accept and appreciate our blended family.

Flexible Holidays

If you're co-parenting and really want to bless your child, you might want to work on developing a trait that has served one mom well. Kay is parenting four children, her husband's two plus her own. I asked her how she manages to cope with all the home pressures during the holidays. Kay responded, "I've learned how to let go. I learned early on that letting the other home have the kids on Christmas Day was not only a gift to my kids, but to myself. . . . I realized that giving them that time helped both homes enjoy the holidays more."

You see, when it comes to her children, Kay has learned how to be flexible. That's rarely an easy thing for anyone to do. And I'm sure she felt quite disappointed that first Christmas Day. But in the end, Kay gave up something she personally wanted for something that everybody needed.

This Christmas season, Lord, help me think less about my personal preferences and more about the needs of those around me and how to make their holiday meaningful.

First and Second Chair

When performing a parenting musical composition, it's important for parents to know their part. For musicians, the honorable first chair generally goes to the most competent player, not necessarily the best one. This musician's long range of experience has taught them how to keep a cool head no matter what happens. They are responsible to lead their section and play the solos.

In a stepfamily, biological parents are first chair on day one. That's because the strength of their relationship and longevity with the child allows them to lead and play the solo moments whenever necessary. The stepparent, on day one, represents second chair. Their role is just as important, but they can gain valuable experience by following the biological parent's lead.

Now, it's important to note that both need to be using the same sheet of parenting music. Their section will sound fuller and blend together more seamlessly when they play in harmony. Especially when they pay attention to their Conductor. That's when the most beautiful music will happen.

Father, as we learn to follow your leading more closely, help each member of our family play their part in developing a beautiful harmony.

Christmas Step-Stress

Here's a tip for managing step-stress during the Christmas holidays: Offer a blessing.

Of course the holidays are wonderful times for children, but they can also be guilt-producing and stressful. Moving between homes usually comes with a mix of emotions. For example, a child may feel sadness for leaving one home, and at the same time feel excited to be with the other family. This is even worse when one home makes the child feel guilty for time spent in the other home.

Instead of making the situation hard for your kids, give them permission to like, love, and enjoy the other household and extended family members. When you say something like "I'm thrilled you're spending time with your dad and stepmom over Christmas. Have lots of fun!" you release them from guilt and from their tendency to worry about you. And you free them to love others and be loved in return. Now, that's a Christmas gift.

Lord, please make me sensitive to the emotions my kids struggle with during holidays. Give me words to say that will free them to fully enjoy their other home and family.

Loving the Wounded Child

Loving a child who has been hurt in the past can be really tough to do. But persevering in love is how you win them over. Out of the goodness of their hearts a great many parents today are attempting to love foster children, adopted children, and stepchildren who have been wounded by people (sometimes family members) or by social systems.

Whatever the cause, sometimes a child's wall goes up and you find it difficult to break down. Here's a thought: Don't try to break down their wall or force your way into their heart. Just hang out, so to speak, as close to their life as you can. Ask about their day, but don't try to get inside their life in areas where they haven't invited you in yet. Support their interests and try to share a smile when they'll let you.

Just accept whatever they give you and love them with the same stubborn love that Jesus lavishes on us. Hey, Christ's love softened your heart. Maybe love can soften theirs, too.

Father God, give me the patience to love from a distance, if necessary, and the words to help heal old wounds.

Everyone Needs a Friend

s one of your holiday traditions watching the movie *It's a Wonderful Life*? One of the most memorable lines is in the last scene, when George Bailey reads a book inscription from Clarence, the angel: "No man is a failure who has friends." Amen to that. If I may, let me add a new twist on that: Someone with friends finds it easier not to be a failure.

Everyone needs someone to just hang out and laugh with. But at one point or another, all of us will need support from friends. We know that life can be really hard at times. We pray and seek God's wisdom and try to rest in his care. But even then, it's good to have a friend standing by you during those tough times.

I see this with blended family couples grappling with stressful circumstances they can't change. If they're able to vent to a friend or small group and find support, they can keep going. And maybe even soar higher than they ever have before. Could you use some more blended family friends?

One final thought: If you aren't already, consider plugging in to a small group or ministry for blended families. And if there isn't one near you, start one. Visit FamilyLife Blended® for the tools you need to get started (FamilyLife.com/blended).

Thank you, Father, for the blessing of friendships and all the ways they enrich our lives.

Giving Our All

What unsung hero comes to mind when you consider the birth of Christ? There are some great choices, but I immediately think of Joseph. In obedience, this carpenter married a woman of questionable reputation and became a father (or is it stepfather or adopted father?) to the Messiah. Joseph had to move away from his family to an unfamiliar place, sacrificing his reputation and career. Then he drifted out of the pages of history.

Faithfully loving and caring for Jesus cost Joseph everything. And then Jesus grew up and taught people that following him costs everything. "Deny yourself and take up your cross," he said (see Matthew 16:24). Joseph certainly understood what that meant. The cost was great for him and it will be for us, too. But the fact is that when we lose ourselves in Jesus, we will find life, just as Joseph did.

So open your heart and receive the Christ child. And give him your all. You'll never regret it.

Lord Jesus, you gave your all for me at the cross. Now I want to give everything I have and all that I am back to you.

Nothing Is Impossible

Holiday pictures should have every family member in the frame, right? Only sometimes, they don't. For lots of families this Christmas, someone will be missing from the portrait. Whether by death or divorce, the joy of the holiday season will be dampened by sadness. In stepfamilies, a family member might be at the other home instead of their usual place at the dinner table. Or tension between family members might be reminding everyone that they aren't quite yet the family they'd like to be.

Be reminded this Christmas season that God has come to his people, bringing hope to the hopeless. Remember that the mercy of Christ helps us love others in spite of tension, disagreements, and conflict. His presence can comfort us in any loss or sorrow. Above all, remember that nothing is impossible with God. Nothing can stop him from carrying out his great plan for our lives.

Humble beginnings and impractical circumstances are not too much for the Almighty to handle. They weren't during that first Christmas, and they certainly aren't now.

Instead of dwelling on what's not perfect about our family, help us focus on the words spoken by Gabriel: "For nothing will be impossible with God" (Luke 1:37).

Holiday Step-Stress Tip: Attend to Loss

H ere's a tip for step-stress at the holidays: Make sure you attend to feelings of loss in children.

The holidays are a bittersweet time for many of us. Perhaps that's related to the traditions and all the good memories of friends and family that also make us keenly aware of what we've lost. I lost my twelve-year-old son in 2009. Of course, I think of him every day, but special days and holidays resurrect my deep sorrow.

Kids in stepfamilies may have this mixed bag of emotions as well. Joy one minute and anger—or should I say, sadness—the next. What they need most during this season is a little extra TLC, and perhaps a little extra grace. Oh, and don't be afraid to comment on the elephant in the room: "I can tell you're missing your mom today. I sure would if I were in your place. And if I were you, I could use an extra hug about now."

Father, help me be aware of feelings of loss and sadness my loved ones struggle with during the holidays. Give me the courage to offer words of comfort.

Viewing Others through God's Eyes

In relationships, do you focus on the good or the bad? Adam faced that choice when God let him choose a name for his wife soon after the couple ate fruit from the forbidden tree. When God had confronted Adam about his disobedience, he blamed it on his wife since she had eaten first. He could have given her a name like One Who Messed Everything Up or Eden Trash. But Adam named his wife Eve, which means "life-giver," even after her actions brought curses on humanity and God's perfect creation.

Bible teacher Tim Lundy says that at that point Adam stopped blaming Eve and looked beyond what he experienced to what God saw in her. He envisioned what God created Eve to be. In faith, he remembered the good and spoke life over his mate.

What if we did that with the people in our life, especially the ones in our home? What if we looked past their bad moments to their intrinsic value and spoke words of life over them?

Father, help me look past the faults and failures of my loved ones to see them with your eyes.

Becoming a Bonus Parent

Bestselling author and stepdad Steve Arterburn shared great ideas on becoming a bonus parent at one of FamilyLife Blended's® Summits on Stepfamily Ministry.

First, while you're dating, don't hang around the kids too much until you're sure the relationship is going somewhere. You don't want the kids attaching to you only to have you stop dating their mom or dad.

Once you get serious and then become their stepparent, be like a benevolent uncle or aunt. Take great interest in their activities. Be positive and encouraging, creating fun experiences for the entire family to enjoy. Try to bond with your stepkids in ways neither of their parents do. Find your unique contribution so you can bring something new and different to their lives.

Finally, demonstrate your love for their parent in obvious ways. Initially kids are invested in their parent's well-being, not necessarily in you, so make sure you take care of their parent. Though not a guarantee, loving their parent makes it more likely they will love you.

Lord, help me discover the unique ways I can enrich my stepchild's life and then share that with them in nonthreatening ways.

Being the Wrong Person Can Be a Good Thing

Have you ever noticed that in God's ministry strategy, the *wrong* person is often the *right* person? If you're like me, there have been times when you felt inadequate and ill-equipped to lead a ministry. "I don't know enough. . . . I haven't lived through this. . . . I don't have the personality for that." These are all things I've told myself at some point.

I hear similar things from couples after I challenge them to start or lead a stepfamily class in their church. "We don't know what we're doing. And besides," they say, "our family hasn't figured it all out yet." And then I say, "That's perfect! Because God's strength is always perfected in your weakness. In God's economy, being the wrong person makes you the right person!"

So how does this work? I like to say it this way: Put yourself in the way of ministry. Just show up and let God work out the rest.

Father, we may not consider ourselves qualified, but we put ourselves at your disposal. Use our family to bless and minister to other stepfamilies even as we trust you to lead and equip us.

The Question of Guardianship

Here's a thought no one wants to entertain: If you and your spouse die, who gets your kids? It might not be pleasant to think about, but if you have minor children you need to settle the answer to that question. One dad just wasn't sure what to do. You see, his wife had died and now he was getting married again. So if he dies, should the new stepmother be the children's guardian, or the people he and his wife had designated long ago?

The question is a relational one; try to answer it from your child's point of view. Who will *they* trust most easily? Who is best positioned to lead, nurture, and provide for them? Initially, the best answer is most likely *not* their stepparent, but it could become so in time.

This isn't about some fantasy family; what's real is what matters here. So base your decision on that, knowing that you can always change it as love grows.

Lord God, help us set aside our reluctance to think about this topic and settle the question according to the best interests of our children.

Choosing Patterns

ere's a question to reflect on: Are you blindly repeating the patterns of the past? As I've gotten older, I've seen more clearly the patterns in my own family—both the ones I want to repeat and the ones I need to avoid. And it seems funny, but even though I've been aware of many of these patterns, I didn't realize how deeply ingrained in me they were.

Sometimes we joke that we become more like our parents as we age, but maybe the reality is that we simply become more aware that we've *always* been like our parents. Even worse, sometimes our spouse tried to tell us that, but we just didn't have ears to hear.

Whether it's a generational family pattern or a behavior you've carried from a previous relationship, it's best to stop shifting the blame to others. Take a good long look in the mirror and then decide: Do I keep it or change it? (And if you decide to change it, turn it into a New Year's resolution—starting tomorrow!)

Lord, help me examine my habits and behavior to determine which patterns I need to discard and which ones are worth keeping.

Notes

1. Joseph Warren Kniskern, Esq., "Remarriage Finances Part 7: Special Financial Issues to Consider Before Remarriage—Estate Planning," Smart Stepfamilies, http://smartstepfamilies.com/view/remarriage-finances-part-7-special-financial-issues-to-consider-before-remarriage--estate-planning.

2. Ron L. Deal and David H. Olson, *The Smart Stepfamily Marriage: Keys to Success in the Blended Family* (Minneapolis: Bethany House, 2015).

3. As quoted in Carroll D. Osburn, *The Peaceable Kingdom: Essays Favoring Non-Sectarian Christianity* (Abilene, TX: Restoration Perspectives, 1993), 127–128.

4. For more on the divorce rate see Shaunti Feldhahn with Tally Whitehead, *The Good News About Marriage: Debunking Discouraging Myths about Marriage and Divorce* (Colorado Springs: Multnomah, 2014), 2–41.

5. The original source of this quotation is unknown, though it has often (on scant evidence) been attributed to Winston Churchill or to George F. Tilton.

6. Read the entire inspirational story in Ron L. Deal, *The Smart Stepfamily* (Minneapolis: Bethany House, 2014), 296–299.

7. Previously unpublished research by Ron Deal and David Olson. For more related research see Ron L. Deal and David H. Olson, *The Smart Stepfamily Marriage*, 105–106.

8. Go to familylife.com/blended for a plan to get you going.

9. Ron L. Deal and David H. Olson, *The Smart Stepfamily Marriage*, 94.

10. Shaunti Feldhahn and Tally Whitehead, *The Good News About Marriage*.

11. Linda J. Waite et al., *Does Divorce Make People Happy? Findings from a Study of Unhappy Marriages* (New York: Institute for American Values, 2002), 5.

12. N.T. Wright, *Surprised by Hope: Rethinking Heaven, the Resurrection, and the Mission of the Church* (New York: HarperCollins, 2008), 288.

13. Ron L. Deal and David H. Olson, *The Smart Stepfamily Marriage*, 32, 136.

14. Ibid., 160.

15. Adapted from Ron L. Deal, "6-Week Summer Sleepover!" Smart Stepfamilies, May 25, 2017, http://smartstepfamilies.com/view/sleepover.

16. Patricia L. Papernow, *Surviving and Thriving in Stepfamily Relationships: What Works and What Doesn't* (New York: Routledge, 2013), 34.

17. Adapted from Ron L. Deal, "6-Week Summer Sleepover!"

18. Ron L. Deal and David H. Olson, *The Smart Stepfamily Marriage*, 185–189.

19. For more on how to do this, read Ron L. Deal, *The Smart Stepfamily* (Minneapolis: Bethany House, 2014).

20. Candice Curry, "An Open Letter to My Daughter's Stepmom," November 30, 2014, https://womenwithworth.wordpress.com/2014/11/30/a-open-letter-to-my-daughters-stepmom.

21. See the research by Scott M. Stanley, PhD, available on his blog, *Sliding vs Deciding*, http://slidingvsdeciding.blogspot.com and summarized here: Scott M. Stanley, Galena K. Rhoades, and Howard J. Markman, "A Summary of Our Work on Cohabitation," (April 2017), https://app.box.com/shared/ugfa85i6lly8hp76qey7. See also Scott M. Stanley, PhD, *The Power of Commitment* (San Francisco: Jossey-Bass, 2005).

22. Sabrina Beasley McDonald, "Learning to 'Speak Marriage' Again," FamilyLife, www.familylife.com/articles/topics/marriage/remarriage/staying-married/learning-to-speak-marriage-again.

23. Adapted from Chris Gonzalez, "Stepfamily Math," Smart Stepfamilies, July 14, 2005, www.smartstepfamilies.com/view/stepfamilymath.

24. Examining your part does not make you responsible for others' behavior. When, for example, they are violent or emotionally abusive, don't blame yourself. Seek safety and counsel about what to do next.

25. For more on this and other principles of good parenting, see Ron L. Deal, *The Smart Stepdad* (Minneapolis: Bethany House, 2011), 119–134.

26. Tianyi Yu and Francesca Adler-Baeder, "The Intergenerational Transmission of Relationship Quality," *Journal of Divorce & Remarriage*, 47:2007, 3, 87–102.

27. Adapted from David Augsburger, *Sustaining Love: Healing and Growth in the Passages of Marriage* (Ventura, CA: Regal, 1988), 55.

28. Forthcoming by Ron L. Deal, David Edwards, and Greg Pettys (2018).

Ron L. Deal is director of FamilyLife Blended®, a division of FamilyLife®, and president of Smart Stepfamilies™. He is a family therapist and sought-after conference speaker specializing in marriage enrichment and stepfamily education. He is one of the most widely read authors on stepfamily living in the country, and his one-minute audio feature *FamilyLife Blended with Ron Deal* can be heard daily on stations nationwide and online.

Ron is author of the Amazon bestselling books *The Smart Stepfamily*, *The Smart Stepfamily Small Group Resource DVD*, *The Smart Stepfamily Participant's Guide*, *The Smart Stepdad*, *Dating and the Single Parent*, *The Smart Stepmom* (with Laura Petherbridge), and *The Smart Stepfamily Marriage* (with Dr. David Olson). He is a member of the Stepfamily Expert Council for the National Stepfamily Resource Center and is a licensed marriage and family therapist and licensed professional counselor.

Ron has extensive experience with the media. He has appeared on dozens of national radio and TV broadcasts in the UK, Canada, Australia, and the US, including Fox News, ABC *Nightline*, WGN-TV News, *FamilyLife Today*, *Chris Fabry Live*, *Family Talk*, and *Focus on the Family*. He has been quoted or referenced by newspapers and publications around the world such as the *New York Times*, *The Wall Street Journal*, ABC News.com, *USA Today*, *U.S. News and World Report*, *Consumer Reports*, and *Ladies Home Journal*.

Ron and his wife, Nan, have three boys and live in Little Rock, Arkansas. Find resources and conference information at RonDeal.org and FamilyLife.com/blended.

Dianne Neal Matthews is the author of four daily devotional books, including *The One Year Women of the Bible* (Tyndale House) and *Designed for Devotion: A 365-Day Journey from Genesis to Revelation* (Baker Books), a 2013 Selah Award winner. She writes regularly for *The Quiet Hour* and has been a contributing writer for Guideposts' *Mornings with Jesus* since the 2013 edition. Her stories and articles have appeared in *LIVE*, *The Christian Communicator*, Focus on the Family periodicals, *Guideposts* magazine, and several compilation books. She has also published Bible studies and newspaper features, and frequently writes guest posts for bloggers and content for websites, including *More to Life* and CBN.com.

Dianne enjoys teaching at writers' conferences, leading Bible studies, and occasionally speaking at women's events. She is a CLASS graduate and a member of Christian Authors Network and Advanced Writers & Speakers Association. She and her husband, Richard, have three grown children and three grandchildren. They currently live in southwest Louisiana. To learn more, please visit DianneNealMatthews.com.

More Vital Blended Family Resources from the Top Name in Stepfamily Ministry!

Visit smartstepfamilies.com and familylife.com/blended for additional information.

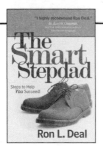

More Resources for the Smart Stepfamily

Visit smartstepfamilies.com and familylife.com/blended for additional information.

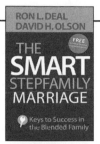

Whether you're dating, engaged, a young stepfamily, or an empty-nest couple, this book will show you how to build on your relationship strengths and improve your weaknesses. Here are the tools you need at any stage to create a remarriage that will last. Includes a free assessment!

The Smart Stepfamily Marriage by Ron L. Deal and David H. Olson

When children are involved, dating gets complicated. In this book, Ron Deal guides single parents—and those who date them—through the emotional ups and downs of dating with kids, including how to navigate relationships, avoid potential pitfalls, and strengthen their families.

Dating and the Single Parent by Ron L. Deal

Ⓑ BETHANYHOUSE